BUILDING INDEPENDENT READERS
A Systematic Approach

Linda Lee & Mary Haymond

▲▼▲

SCHOLASTIC

New York · Toronto · London · Auckland · Sydney
Mexico City · New Delhi · Hong Kong · Buenos Aires

Acknowledgments:

We thank our editor, Sarah Glasscock, for her expert guidance along the way and development editor, Joanna Davis-Swing, for believing our manuscript was worthy of publication. A special acknowledgement goes to the many mentors and colleagues who have inspired and guided us throughout our careers. And finally, we wish to recognize Lou Haymond for helping us make our work better.

Cover design by Jorge J. Namerow
Cover photograph: © MediaBakery
Interior design by Teresa B. Southwell
Interior photographs by the authors.
Development editor: Joanna Davis-Swing
Editor: Sarah Glasscock

ISBN: 978-0-545-32963-7

CONTENTS

FOREWORD

Linda Lee and Mary Haymond propose to build independent readers. They move beyond a clarion call for independent reading to offer rich guidance for its use. Like others, they teach literacy with love and wisdom. This goal is important for teachers and these political times.

Linda and Mary offer clearly articulated proposals for building independent readers. They accompany detailed and representative instructional plans with personal classroom examples. They take on the multifaceted challenge of artfully blending their proposals with theoretical and empirical rationales while making them doable. This account of their practices combined with classroom anecdotes evidences deep caring along with a delight and confidence in their students. Their sensitively chosen language is a testament to their heartfelt respect for the diverse students whom they serve and their deep belief that all students can become accomplished and independent readers. Teachers and others who care about the reading achievement of our nation's youth will benefit from the straightforward messages as well as the more subtle examples this book holds.

Linda and Mary boldly devote a large amount of their language arts time for their students to read. This time allotment matters since the chance to read a wide range of books, while providing the best practice, seldom occurs. In today's world, teachers often face increased testing that competes with instruction, mandated practices that replace professional prerogatives, and the purchase of published programs over an investment in books for real reading. These realities often lead to a substitution of things to do (what Linda and Mary call "stuff") for real reading. In some classrooms, independent reading is considered a luxury for some rather than a cornerstone for all. This book shows how teachers can (and should) devote large chunks of time to reading. The authors do this without forsaking students' instructional needs or setting aside the state and national standards for which all teachers are accountable. In their classrooms, the goal of reading encompasses a rich, accurate, and personalized grasp of a text that places books center stage. Their use of books offers a basis for their students' cognitive and affective growth, a critical blending of an ability and desire to read. Importantly, instruction accompanies each step along the way. Linda and Mary explain the important role of word identification strategies and how to develop them within an attention to comprehension. They don't assume that deep understanding automatically follows quick and accurate identification of words, so they carefully address comprehension. They demonstrate what it is like to create a joyful learning environment for teachers and students. Students read, share their successes, help their peers, and read better. As their teachers, Linda and Mary personalize instructional guidance along the way.

Teachers who care about their students' reading achievement desire to promote an ability to read, a willingness to read, and the pure enjoyment of reading across a lifetime. Linda and Mary have dedicated their long and successful careers to these goals. These authors value research as a basis for the ideas that they implement, and they remain learners, something readers will value even more in the wonderful pages that follow. This book will undoubtedly reinforce the power of real reading and the importance of an instructional guide, a teacher, to harness the potential for all students to read with confidence and enthusiasm.

My comments about this book capture my sentiments as a former teacher and current teacher educator and researcher. I now take a more personal turn and acknowledge my good fortune in knowing Linda and Mary. I have visited their classrooms on numerous occasions, witnessed firsthand their interactions with students, enjoyed the welcoming classrooms that they created, and marveled at their students' abilities to explain their books' content and their reading strategies. I have seen them implement the ideas and tap the language promoted and used in this book. I have interacted with them as participants in my research and members of a Language and Literacy Collaborative while at Washington State University. And, we have spent hours and hours together exploring literacy issues and instructional directions. I continue to learn so much with and from them. So, I celebrate their completion of this text and the opportunity it affords other teachers and stakeholders to learn from their important example. They are scholars who remain classroom teachers and who choose to teach in a school with children from all walks of life. They contend with issues and challenges shared by teachers nationwide. They persevere. Their students read.

When I ended my reading of this book, I was left with hope and gratitude. I hold hope that the suggestions in it will rekindle a commitment to independent reading as the essential ingredient for all students' reading achievement. I also hope that more teachers will be emboldened and empowered to hold independent reading not only as their primary goal but also as their students' main activity during language arts period. I am grateful that Linda and Mary chose to share their good ideas and serve as professional mentors.

Our young people should learn to read with joy, receive guidance along the way, and develop a life-long reading habit. Linda and Mary do much to promote this vision. So, sit back, read, turn the pages, learn, think, and enjoy.

~ **Mary F. Roe, Ph.D.**
Professor
Arizona State University

INTRODUCTION

How do we foster the habits and skills that young students need to be productive and enthusiastic during independent reading time?

Over the years, we have hosted hundreds of visitors to our readers' workshop, and the most common question they ask is always, "How do you get your children to stay happily engaged with reading for so long?" It is such an important and worthy question, and this book, reflecting research-based best practices, is our attempt to answer it. Our purpose is to help teachers craft an independent reading time where all children grow into productive and passionate readers.

If you had visited our classrooms 12 years ago during independent reading time, you would have seen something entirely different: a few children would be reading, some would be completing artistic responses, others would be filling in book logs, while still others would be working at a variety of centers. Our goal then was to keep students busy while we did our small-group work or conferred with individuals. We didn't consider the implications of having our children do "stuff" rather than the real work of reading.

As we read and studied research-based best practices, we were struck by the power of this statement: "In less-effective classrooms, there is a lot of stuff going on for which no reliable evidence exists to support their use (e.g., test-preparation workbooks, playing with magnetic letters at a center, completing after-reading comprehension worksheets)." (Allington, 2002). We took a close look at the "stuff" our students were doing and realized that we needed to build in more time for reading and that we still lacked a vision for how to make this happen.

Opportunities to visit Debbie Miller's classroom in Denver and Sharon Taberski's classroom at the Manhattan New School gave us the vision we needed to transition from facilitating reading-related stuff to real reading. Debbie Miller taught and learned from children in the Denver Public Schools for 30 years; Sharon Taberski was a classroom teacher for 28 years. In both classroom settings, it was clear that six- to eight-year-old children were capable of reading for extended periods of time. After a reading workshop mini-lesson, children grabbed their book bags and went off to read. Their reading stamina allowed these classroom teachers to do group work and confer with kids. Neither Debbie nor Sharon needed to spend time managing the room because the children were independently doing the work of real reading. They weren't just doing stuff! This was what we envisioned for our students, and once we saw it in action, we were committed to making it happen in our own classrooms.

If you visited our classrooms today, you would see children scattered around the room reading independently, reading with a partner, reading with a group, and talking about books. They would be doing what real readers do . . . pursuing interests, engaging in lively discussions, and becoming lost in the flow of reading.

Students engaged in independent reading

In this book, we explore the six essential components embedded in the readers' workshop that form an independent reading program:

- ✿ The gradual release of responsibility instructional model
- ✿ Community
- ✿ Book choice
- ✿ Fix-up strategies
- ✿ Talk
- ✿ Summary

To create the conditions necessary to foster engaged and passionate readers, you must understand the components. The first part of our book will define each of them and then fit the pieces of the puzzle together in the lesson plans in the second section. Use the 30 lessons in our book to establish the foundation of your independent reading workshop during the first six weeks of school. Most of the lessons, except for a few on fix-up strategies, have this easy-to-follow format to help guide your instruction:

- ✿ Teaching point
- ✿ Weekly conversation skill focus
- ✿ Materials list and preparation notes
- ✿ Activating prior knowledge
- ✿ Modeling the lesson
- ✿ Focusing the conversation
- ✿ Restating the teaching point
- ✿ Moving to independent practice
- ✿ Independent reading practice
- ✿ Share circle

This is how to build an engaging and productive independent reading workshop that will help you support and inspire passionate and lifelong readers.

~ Linda Lee & Mary Haymond

CHAPTER 1:
Teaching Reading in the Early Grades

Many books have been written about what and how to teach young readers, but we struggled to find a comprehensive resource that provided a description of how to build independent readers who were passionate about books. Most resources encouraged us to have young readers spend their independent reading time working at centers or reading books from their group work. These recommendations may teach children to read, but they do little to foster a love of reading. Over time, we found a few key practices that helped us build the foundation for a successful independent reading program.

- ✮ First, we established goals for our early readers that would serve as a guide for our day-to-day practice.
- ✮ Next, we organized our reading program in a way that facilitated large blocks of time for independent reading. Readers' workshop is the model we used.
- ✮ Then, we implemented teaching approaches designed to slowly build toward independence.
- ✮ Finally, we incorporated strategies for teaching students how to have conversations about books during share circle.

GOALS FOR EARLY READERS

Before you can set up a successful independent reading program, you need to consider the long-term goals you have for your students. We had the opportunity to learn from Margaret Mooney, a noted New Zealand teacher educator. Her work became the guiding force in helping us design our independent reading time. We developed long-term goals for readers based on the hallmarks of a reader as defined by Mooney.

Long-Term Goals for Readers

- ✮ Views reading as a meaning-making process
- ✮ Reads and reflects
- ✮ Rereads books
- ✮ Reads for pleasure and information
- ✮ Reads widely
- ✮ Encourages others to read
- ✮ Is interested in hearing about books
- ✮ Can set own purpose for reading
- ✮ Is motivated to read
- ✮ Initiates own reading activity
- ✮ Makes time to read outside of school
- ✮ Views reading as worthwhile

READERS' WORKSHOP USING THE GRADUAL RELEASE OF RESPONSIBILITY INSTRUCTIONAL MODEL

Once we established long-term goals, the readers' workshop model provided the necessary structure to help us build independent readers. Readers' workshop is used to organize the teaching approaches in the gradual release of responsibility instructional model (Pearson & Gallagher, 1983). This model is the method recommended for explicitly teaching comprehension strategies so readers are able to understand and remember what they have read. We have also applied the gradual release model to teach students how to figure out tricky words so they can read independently. Fielding and Pearson (1994) identified four components for instruction that follow the gradual release model.

1. Model one teaching point at a time using a read-to or shared-reading approach.
2. Guide students in practicing the teaching point using small-group work or individual conferences.
3. Provide large amounts of time for students to practice using and applying what they have learned.
4. Use assessment tools and data to develop the pace of instruction for students.

TEACHING PRACTICES THAT BUILD INDEPENDENCE

The gradual release of responsibility instructional model is only effective when children are provided with large amounts of time to practice what you have taught. In order to accommodate an extended independent reading time block, the reading workshop is divided into three parts:

✯ Mini-lesson
✯ Independent reading
✯ Share circle

Share Circle: 10 minutes

Mini-Lesson: 10-15 minutes

Independent Reading: 45-50 minutes

Reader's Workshop Wheel

▶The Mini-Lesson

As the circle graph shows, reading workshop begins with a 10- to 15-minute mini-lesson. During the mini-lesson, the gradual release of responsibility instructional model is used to explicitly teach what students are going to learn. Read-to or shared-reading are the teaching approaches used during mini-lessons.

↗ Read-To Teaching Approach

In the gradual release of responsibility instructional model, reading to students is the first approach you use in a mini-lesson. The purpose of reading to students is to demonstrate your teaching point. Here is a sample introduction to a mini-lesson on easy books:

> *Today, I am going to teach you what makes a book easy to read. Readers read easy books to build fluency and because it is fun. You know when a book is easy for you because you can read all the words, you sound like a storyteller, and you remember what you have read. Watch, listen, and think about my reading to see if this book is easy for me.*

We carefully select the text for our demonstration so the lesson is short and focused on the teaching point. When teaching a read-to mini-lesson, we begin by telling students what we are going to teach and how it helps readers. Then we use a think-aloud to demonstrate the teaching point. During the mini-lesson, students are responsible for watching, listening, and thinking, but they are not yet expected to apply their developing knowledge independently.

↗ Shared-Reading Teaching Approach

After a few read-to mini-lessons on a teaching point, we support students' growth toward independence by transitioning to a shared-reading lesson. Students move from watching and listening to the lesson to sharing and following along. The lesson format is similar to a read-to, but the difference is in the transfer of some responsibility to students. Now they have the opportunity to share their thinking and observations about what is being taught. Here's a sample introduction to a shared-reading mini-lesson on easy books:

> *Today, I am going to review what makes a book easy to read. Readers read easy books to build fluency and because it is fun. You know when a book is easy for you because you can read all the words, you sound like a storyteller, and you remember what you have read. Watch, listen, and think about my reading today because I am not sure if this book is easy for me. When I finish reading the text, you are going to turn and talk to your partner and decide if the book was easy for me. I am going to need your advice, so please listen carefully as I read.*

▶ Talk

A variety of techniques is used during shared-reading mini-lessons to involve all students in thinking and discussing what's being taught. One technique is thinking partners. Partners sit side-by-side at each lesson and turn and talk when given a signal. Sometimes, we assign a letter, A or B, to each partner. When a question is posed for discussion, partner A may be instructed to respond first. Partner B listens until it is his or her turn to share. While pairs are talking, we listen in to as many conversations as possible to try to capture snippets that would be beneficial to share with the whole group. When there seems to be a lull in the conversation, we ask a few of the partners we identified to share their thinking. Teaching the art of conversation is presented throughout the mini-lesson plans on pages 54–125.

We have used two books as mentor texts on teaching conversation: *Comprehension Through Conversation: The Power of Purposeful Talk in the Reading Workshop* by Maria Nichols (Heinemann, 2006) and *Knee to Knee, Eye to Eye: Circling in on Comprehension* by Ardith Davis Cole (Heinemann, 2003). Their valuable ideas on how to teach children to engage in purposeful talk are integrated into our lesson plans.

Several lessons are required to effectively teach students how to engage in purposeful talk. Again, using the gradual release of responsibility instructional model allows you to give children many opportunities to watch demonstrations and practice using talk to further their learning.

These are the six conversational moves that we teach over time:

1. Use appropriate body language
2. Listen and paraphrase
3. Listen and agree
4. Listen, agree, and add on with more evidence from the text
5. Listen and disagree, providing evidence from the text
6. Listen and ask questions to clarify meaning

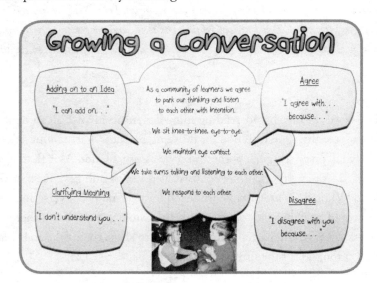

Classroom chart for growing a conversation

Charts

We use charts during the mini-lessons. As part of the process, we tell our students that writing things down is a way people keep a record of their thinking, and it helps them remember important information. In an effort to connect daily teaching and learning, we co-construct charts with children. These charts provide a written record of teaching points that we, the teachers, and our students can refer to over time. Charts document previous teaching and learning, and they serve as reminders of what has come before so that students can connect to what is to come. To create a truly beneficial chart, record a descriptor of what is being taught as a header. Each day, add the teaching point that you will introduce during the lesson. The chart is used during the explanation portion of a mini-lesson to activate prior knowledge and to state the new learning. At the beginning of each subsequent mini-lesson, we read the entire chart. This simple routine activates prior knowledge and sets the purpose for the lesson.

INDEPENDENT READING

After a reading workshop mini-lesson, children need time to read independently. Simply reading itself is a powerful contributor to the development of accurate, fluent, high-comprehension reading. Children need time to practice and consolidate the strategies and skills they have learned from mini-lessons, small-group work, and reading conferences. They also need to spend time with books so they fall in love with reading. When students are not working with us individually or in a small group, they are reading and responding to text. Sometimes they are reading with a partner or in a small group. The goal is to establish a routine so that students can work without much assistance and are engaged in reading a text that, most of the time, is at their independent reading level.

Again, children need to spend large amounts of time reading in order to become good readers. In our reading workshops, students are reading independently for 45–50 minutes a day. In order to help children achieve reading independence, we must ensure the following:

- ✵ They have a wide range of reading material from which to choose.
- ✵ They understand how to select books.
- ✵ They possess a purpose for reading.
- ✵ They use decoding and comprehension strategies.
- ✵ They know classroom expectations.
- ✵ They have time to practice.

We spend the first six weeks of the school year working on the routines and behaviors that enable students to want to sustain their reading. Some of the routines and behaviors we teach in mini-lessons include how to make appropriate book choices, how to linger with a text, and what to do after finishing a book.

▶Responding to Reading

During the mini-lessons, we teach students how to "hold their thinking" by coding text with sticky notes, using double-entry diaries, and writing in their Thinking Journals. Teaching them the importance of recording their thinking is much more authentic than filling out a worksheet. It also gives a purpose to the reading work they are doing during independent reading time. Recording thinking with the goal of sharing it with others is very motivational. It helps young readers build stamina.

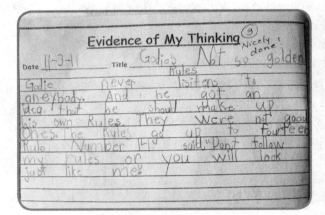
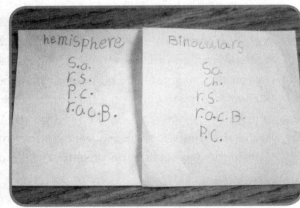

Student responses in Thinking Journals and double-entry diaries

▶Individual and Group Work

As students are independently reading, we work with individuals and small groups. Our role is to serve as a guide on the side while students try to explore as readers. We provide regular feedback during this time. Here are some teaching approaches we use for individual and group work:

- � Individualized reading conference
- ✧ Shared-reading/strategy group
- ✧ Guided reading
- ✧ Literature circle
- ✧ Literature circle and book club

Individualized Reading Conference: We work with individual students to support them as they develop as readers. The child is doing the reading work; we act as coaches.

As a student and teacher hold a conference, the rest of the class is engaged in reading.

 Building Independent Readers © 2012 by Linda Lee & Mary Haymond • Scholastic Teaching Resources

Shared-Reading/Strategy Group: Children are grouped together based on a common need. We model a strategy, and students participate by interacting with our demonstration. Students are then asked to apply what they have seen demonstrated to the text they are reading. They are not all reading the same text.

Guided Reading: We work with a small group of students, supporting them as they make meaning from text. Students are selected on the basis of similar instructional needs. They are all reading the same text, and we serve as a guide on the side.

The teacher listens to students' responses in a guided reading group.

Literature Circle and Book Club: In a literature circle, we work with a small group of students to help them learn how to think critically about a text and how to negotiate meaning through conversation. Students can also create book clubs and run them effectively if they have been taught the elements that make book clubs successful.

SHARE CIRCLE

A share circle follows independent reading time. All readers need to share their reading with others, and a share circle facilitates this. The mini-lesson plans in this book include a guide on how to get students to actively talk and listen to each other. Instead of having the teacher in charge of the discussion, the focus is on children listening and learning from each other. The purpose of share circle is to do the following:

- ✫ Celebrate reading successes
- ✫ Share how children applied what you taught in the mini-lesson to the text they were reading and explain how it helped their comprehension
- ✫ Communicate what students learned from reading
- ✫ Show that students understand and can remember what they have read
- ✫ Validate ideas and the ability to problem solve
- ✫ Share evidence of reaching a goal

Students sit in a large circle during this activity. The student who is sharing stands up, and the expectation is that all eyes will be on the speaker and not the teacher. The person sharing needs to be taught how to address the group, and our mini-lesson plans address that. Another way to organize sharing is to have children sit facing an easel. In this case, the speaker stands in front of the group.

Not everyone will have an opportunity to share every day. One way to facilitate talk about text is to give your students a few minutes to "buzz" with their partner about the reading work they just completed. This time provides an opportunity for all voices to be heard and gives purpose to the reading work done during independent reading time.

ASSESSMENT

We collect evidence of student understanding and application with the following assessment tools:

- ✯ A quick running record using a just-right text the child is reading to determine future teaching point(s)
- ✯ Small-group work
- ✯ Reading conferences
- ✯ Mini-lesson interactions and conversations
- ✯ Independent-reading time observations
- ✯ Book logs
- ✯ Share circle
- ✯ Sticky notes
- ✯ Thinking Journals

This assessment data helps us determine when most of our students are ready for new learning. For example, assessment data can help us determine when most of our students have built reading stamina, possess a range of fix-up strategies, can choose easy, interesting, and just-right books, and can summarize text. We always have some students who are in need of more instructional time with fix-up strategies, book choice, and summary, but we facilitate their learning during small-group work. Assessment data also serves as a guide for the pacing of our lesson plans throughout the year.

Having clear goals in mind and using a reading workshop to implement the gradual release of responsibility creates the foundation for building an independent reading program. During independent reading time, teachers are busy teaching and students are busy reading. Students have a focus for their reading work. They are reading and showing evidence that they can figure out tricky words, summarize what they are reading, and make wise book choices. The next chapter explains how to empower students to choose their own reading material.

● ● ●

Building Independent Readers © 2012 by Linda Lee & Mary Haymond • Scholastic Teaching Resources

CHAPTER 2:
Book Choice

To illustrate the importance of book choice, we offer the following anecdote from Mary:

At the beginning of independent reading time, Jacob rushed over to me and repeatedly poked my arm. When I turned to ask him to stop, his expression told me it wasn't the time to discuss a less annoying way to attract attention. I knelt down and listened as he said, "I really need to talk to you about book choice. I've read all the books in my book bag twice already this week, and when I look around the room and see all the great books, it makes me feel so sad. If I only get to pick out six books a week, there are books in here I'll never get to read. So, can I please pick out new books every two days instead of just six for the week?"

I couldn't believe my ears. This was a total shift in attitude for Jacob. He had come to school six weeks earlier reluctant to even pick up one book. His demeanor during the independent reading portion of readers' workshop told me that he believed reading was not for him, and there was nothing in the world anyone could do to change his mind. He spent the first two weeks roaming the room, fussing about finding books at his level, and spending way too much time in the restroom. What magic had occurred during those first six weeks of school? How was I able to help Jacob become internally motivated to read? I believe it was the power of choice!

Jacob had entered the classroom in September as an older student in my multi-age setting. He had already experienced a year of first grade at another school, and now, as a second grader, displayed an alarming lack of interest in reading. As I looked through the information sent by his previous school, I decided to call his teacher to gain insights into his lack of interest in reading. His first-grade teacher said that Jacob left first grade reading on grade level. She went on to describe her reading program, and as she finished, the pieces of his puzzling behavior began to fit together. He had come from a school where he was only allowed to read leveled books assigned to him. When Jacob wasn't in a guided-reading group reading his leveled books, he spent time at an assigned literacy center. A small amount of time during the day was provided for independent reading, but again, he was limited to reading the leveled books he had practiced during his group time. Jacob was not allowed to read books that were not at his level. When I asked about his reading interests, his teacher had to admit that she really had no idea.

No wonder Jacob had entered my classroom with an attitude that reading wasn't for him! Yes, he had learned to read, but he hadn't developed an interest in reading. Book choice was the missing element.

WHY OFFERING CHOICE IS ESSENTIAL

In *What Really Matters for Struggling Readers,* Richard Allington states that the evidence is clear: greater choice enhances academic engagement and reading achievement. Choice of reading material not only empowers children with a sense of ownership, but it also stimulates engagement in the reading process. If we want students to value reading and become independent readers, we must give them the opportunity to choose most of what they read. However, the process of choice can be overwhelming for a child. Books come in a multitude of topics and levels of difficulty. Therefore, it is vital that we give children the tools to make appropriate choice.

TEACHING BOOK CHOICE

Over time, Mary taught Jacob how to choose books, and as his confidence grew, he started to view himself as a reader. She knew that teaching him how to make good book selections was the obvious place to begin. We start by teaching the three categories of books to all our children:

- ✩ **Easy** for fluency practice
- ✩ **Just right** for strategy application
- ✩ **Interesting**—which may be easy, just right, or a bit challenging—but are of interest to the reader

Book choice instruction begins by teaching easy books. This ensures that most students will be successful. Then teach students how to choose interesting books so they can build reading stamina by lingering over books with topics of high interest. Introduce just-right books last so there will be time to teach and/ or review the fix-up strategies. After teaching all three categories of books, ask children to warm up by reading their easy books, followed by their just-right books, and finally have them cool down by reading their interesting books.

▶ Easy Books

From Richard Allington's recommendations about the type of text needed for independent reading, we understand the importance of reading books that are easy so students can practice fluency and expression and understand them. Again, we teach how to choose easy books first because most of our students have immediate success. High-success reading is absolutely critical to reading development and to creating a positive attitude toward reading.

Mary's anecdote continues: *I started by teaching Jacob and his classmates the characteristics of an easy book:*

- ✩ *You can read all the words.*
- ✩ *You sound like a storyteller.*
- ✩ *You understand and remember what you have read.*

I explained that reading easy books is important to a reader because it helps build fluency and expression. I modeled reading easy books, and my demonstrations included teaching the term fluency *by comparing it to reading like a storyteller. I also explained that reading an easy book is like the warm-up exercises the children do in health and fitness. The exercises are designed to get their muscles ready for the games and activities to follow. The same is true when they read easy books; their brains are getting ready for the work to follow. I spent five lessons modeling how to choose easy books, and I invited students to select their own easy books after each lesson, offering support to individuals and small groups as needed.*

When it was time for Jacob to practice finding and reading easy books, he went through the motions, and this was when I first observed his avoidance behaviors. Even though there were many books in the classroom that were easy for him, Jacob would only pick up books, flip through the pages, and then put them away. He was constantly on the move and never seemed to find anything satisfying. He fussed about not finding books at his level and worked hard to avoid reading. I knew the basket of Mo Willems' books just might provide the motivation and humor to hook Jacob on reading. They would be easy for him and of high interest. Jacob tried to argue that the books weren't on his level, but his concerns gave way to laughter as I read part of There's a Bird on Your Head! *to him. He quickly grabbed the book out of my hand, selected another by Mo Willems, and headed to a table to read. I watched Jacob devour both books and then go to the basket to gather more Mo Willems books to read. His journey to becoming an intrinsically motivated reader had begun.*

▶Interesting Books

After we observe that most of our students are capable of selecting easy books, we introduce interesting books. These books can be at any instructional level but are of high interest to the student. Children can get meaning from viewing the pictures and using other text features. Most important, they are engaged and want to linger with the book for a long time. Interesting books are introduced second because, again, all children will be successful. Also, by introducing interesting books second, we find that students are happy to look at a variety of books for longer periods of time, which builds their reading stamina.

Nonfiction tends to be the type of text children select for their interesting book choice because they have a natural curiosity about the world. We foster this sense of wonder by having nonfiction texts with fascinating topics and amazing photographs in our classrooms. Over time, our mini-lessons include demonstrations on how to get information from nonfiction text by "viewing" the photographs, illustrations, labels, captions, and other text features. The goal is to teach children how to view and learn from nonfiction texts when they may not be able to read all the words. Learning how to view nonfiction text is critical to reading development and is not to be confused with "fake" reading. Our entry point into teaching how to read nonfiction is through imagery. How many times have you purchased a magazine and spent your time looking at the pictures and reading the captions? As with easy books, we offer support to students who need help finding interesting books.

When teaching interesting book choice, we return to the comparison to health and fitness. After exercising our muscles, we need time to cool them down. Reading an interesting book during the last portion of independent reading time allows students' brains to cool down after the effort they exerted reading their just-right books. Again, once book choice is fully operational, we ask children to read their easy books first, just-right books second, and interesting books last. Let's return to Mary's anecdote about Jacob to demonstrate this:

After children had time to practice choosing interesting books, I started to see their level of engagement rise. I took advantage of this by spending crucial time getting to know my students and their unique interests. I watched as they browsed for books and I began teaching them how to locate books that satisfied their passion for learning. This is when I helped them shop for the perfect book. Reading became an authentic activity—children learned how to pay attention to their own interests and felt valued in the classroom setting. When they took their books and started reading, they began to demonstrate stamina and endurance—the ability to do something for a long period of time. They became highly focused on their special interests and were often unaware of the passage of time. When I gathered students together at share circle, I honored those who were in the "flow" by blowing bubbles on them. Then I asked them to describe what made it possible for them to read the entire time. The discussion motivated all of my readers to "fall in love" with reading.

When it was time to practice selecting interesting texts, I questioned Jacob about his interests. I soon discovered he had a passion for snakes. I directed him to the basket of nonfiction books about reptiles. Even though some of the material was too hard for Jacob to read independently, I encouraged him to pick out books he could linger with for a long time. I was confident the text would help Jacob build the reading stamina and endurance he so needed. He sat at a table and pored over his books until it was time to gather at the carpet for share circle. Jacob couldn't wait to share a photograph of a snake eating a mouse. He read the caption to help explain what he had learned from viewing the photograph. What a change from the prior two weeks! Jacob was engaged with the material because he was given choice, and reading had become a purposeful and enjoyable activity. I taught two lessons on how to select interesting books, and my students quickly demonstrated they understood why and how to choose books in this category.

▶ Just-Right Books

The last category of books we introduce is just-right books. We spend the majority of the reader's workshop time at the beginning of the year teaching students fix-up strategies and how to monitor for meaning at the word and sentence levels. By the time we are ready to introduce just-right books, all the students have had some fix-up strategies they could apply when they encountered unfamiliar words. We devote the greatest amount of instructional time to teaching just-right books because students read those for most of their independent reading time.

A book is "just right" when a child can read most of the words, use fix-up strategies to figure out unknown words, and meaning is maintained. While teaching the category of just-right books, we talk about the brain and what learners can do to make their intelligence grow. Just as in health and fitness, once they have warmed up their muscles (easy books), they use those muscles to do an activity. The brain is like a muscle, and every time a reader uses it to solve a problem (e.g., figuring out a tricky word), it becomes stronger. It forms new connections, and this makes students smarter. When students are reading just-right books, their brains are working hard to solve tricky words and make meaning. Through this effort and the new connections made, the brain gets stronger—and students get smarter.

Mary explains how Jacob responded to choosing just-right books:

By the time I introduced the category of just-right books, Jacob was hooked on reading. He understood the purpose of reading easy books and would gladly practice reading his easy books first. When he was finished, he would say, "My brain is fired up, and now I am ready to read my just-right books." Jacob selected two just-right books. After finishing them, he would linger over his interesting books, gaining information from viewing the photographs, reading the captions, labels, and diagrams, and utilizing other supportive features of text. After six weeks of lessons on book choice, Jacob had developed a positive stance toward reading. He displayed an understanding of why and how to choose books in each category and was fully engaged during independent reading time.

Classroom Book Choice chart

 Building Independent Readers © 2012 by Linda Lee & Mary Haymond • Scholastic Teaching Resources

SCAFFOLDING FOR STUDENTS HAVING TROUBLE WITH BOOK CHOICE

As we observe our students, we watch carefully for individuals who are having difficulty choosing books. We try hard to uncover the cause of their hesitation or anxiety. Are they afraid their choice will be denigrated by others? Are they afraid we might uncover some weakness? Are they coming from a classroom where choice was never allowed? Responding positively to their approximations is the first step toward supporting students having difficulty choosing books. We also help them shop for a perfect book by discovering their interests and helping them find books on that topic. Children learn how to pay attention to their own interests and feel valued in the classroom setting.

Human Learning Continuum Activity

Fundamental to the success of book choice is teaching students to develop an appreciation for their individual differences. An effective activity for doing this is building a "human learning continuum." We invite five or six children to line up from novice to expert according to their knowledge of a recreational activity, such as soccer, fishing, karate, playing the piano, and so on. We do not use academic subjects for this activity. We privately ask those students with the most academic challenges what they are an expert on and use it as one of the activity topics. At least two different topics are presented, and we point out how each child's placement changed on the continuum. We discuss the factors that influence each child's place on the learning continuum (opportunities to learn, access to required materials, assistance from a knowledgeable other, and interest in the activity). Upon completing the activity, we discuss the continuum in comparison to reading. Students come to understand that we are all at different points on that learning continuum, and we need to honor individual differences. As we grow as learners and readers, and give each other encouragement and support, our place on the continuum will change.

As we build a strong sense of a reading community in the classroom, children find it easier to take a risk as they self-select their own reading materials. The fear of being judged—because of the number of pages in their book or their reading level—soon disappears since a sense of trust has been fostered. Students understand that everyone is at a different place on the learning continuum and that we are all responsible for supporting each other on this journey.

Emergent Readers

To support emergent readers as they begin to make book selections, we provide tubs of leveled books that are identified by colored dots. Our system requires only four tubs of leveled books. This allows us to suggest a place in the room where some of our readers can find an easy book. This scaffolding helps ensure that students feel successful with book choice at the very beginning of the school year. Approximation will be part of initial book choice, but with guided-reading groups and lots of practice, students will successfully select books from each of the three categories. In this way, we are helping our readers develop the skills necessary to make appropriate book choices.

Colored dots identify leveled books in tubs.

When most of the class is looking for books, we gather our emergent readers who need the most support and help them find easy books. The orange dot tub is often used because it contains books that have patterned and predictable text. We may read aloud a text to children and then provide each of them with a copy so they can read it independently.

▶English Language Learners

We also strive to have books available that reflect the cultural identity of each of our students. Honoring and understanding the community that they are a part of can help us win students' trust and help them discover all that we can about them as individual learners. Only then will students be active participants in our classroom.

We also understand that silence is normal for an English Language Learner. Making sure book choice comes with low anxiety is accomplished by honoring approximation. Most of the books ELLs choose initially might fit under the interesting book category, and this should be accepted. Choice provides the motivation these students often need to learn and to actively participate in independent reading. Over time, they will acquire the knowledge and language necessary to make wise book choices.

CLASSROOM LIBRARIES

Richard Allington (2006) states that the research is clear: children need daily access to rich supplies of engaging, accessible, appropriate books so they can develop as thoughtful, eager, and engaged readers.

- ✫ Higher achieving schools had more books in classroom library collections than lower achieving schools did.
- ✫ Schools in wealthier neighborhoods had classrooms with larger book collections than schools in poorer neighborhoods.
- ✫ Classrooms with a larger supply of books had kids who read more frequently.
- ✫ Classrooms with a larger supply of books usually had more kids reading books they could read successfully.

Most teachers are not supplied with books, and they spend years creating book collections using their own money. No wonder they have to resort to using literacy centers or other "stuff" to keep their children busy while they work with groups. Without a well-stocked classroom library, children are not able to choose what to read and practice reading independently.

Many of our schools have spent money to stock book rooms with multiple copies of leveled texts, but the resources are used for guided-reading groups or book clubs. That's well and good, but building classroom libraries also needs to be a priority. Few classroom libraries meet the American Librarian Association's guidelines of a minimum of 20–25 books per child.

Most teachers believe creating a classroom library is of the utmost importance, so they go to garage sales, library book sales, join the Scholastic Book Club, and ask their parent-teacher groups to hold fundraisers to purchase books for classrooms. We recommend that you use the research in presenting a case for making wise decisions about available funding in your district to create classroom libraries.

▶Organizing a Classroom Library

There are resources available that can guide you in organizing a classroom library, arranging books by level of difficulty without assigning a level, and providing a list of recommended books. Our favorite resource is the *Beyond Leveled Books: Supporting Early and Transitional Readers in Grades K–5* by Karen Szymusiak, Franki Sibberson, and Lisa Koch (Stenhouse, 2008). Their book explores the uses and limitations of leveled texts in primary reading instruction. It also suggests a system for creating and organizing baskets of books.

Fiction classroom library

Nonfiction classroom library

After level 20, we don't level our books. Our classrooms are filled with a variety of mini-libraries for children to access. We created our nonfiction library by sorting nonfiction books into piles according to topic. Then we assigned each topic to a basket. The basket has a label with a letter written on it, and all the books that belong in the basket have that same number written on them. The same process was used to create our fiction library.

We also have a book club library that uses baskets. Each basket contains at least four copies of the same title. As the year progresses, self-selected groups of children use the resources when they partner read or form small book clubs.

Baskets are scattered around the room with books organized by favorite authors, funny books, friendship, fairy tales, poetry, biographies, predictable text, song books, ABC books, and a host of series books ranging from Little Bear to the Magic Tree House. A variety of picture books are also displayed on the window ledge for children to select. Many of those books have been used in a read-aloud or a mini-lesson.

Books are organized in baskets and displayed on window ledges.

RELEASING RESPONSIBILITY TO STUDENTS

For two days each week, we continue to teach mini-lessons to our children about book choice. Eventually the book choice lessons are reduced to one day each week. During these mini-lessons, we read books from the classroom libraries to show students where to find books that fit the book choice category we are investigating. Students are given lots of time to practice choosing books in each of the categories.

When most of our children understand how to choose books, we give them a book bag and ask them to choose two books from each category. Students are expected to choose their books on Monday and keep reading them until Friday. By this time, we have repeatedly modeled the value and enjoyment we get from rereading books, so asking our students to stay with the same five or six books for a week is not a problem. Children begin by reading their easy books to build fluency. Next, they read their just right-books to practice their fix-up strategies and get better at reading. Then they read their interesting books.

At the beginning of the school year, the independent reading practice is approximately 20–30 minutes. If we need to shorten the length of independent work time, we do. It all depends upon the children. Our goal is to make sure they are successful during independent reading time.

A students' book bag

As the year progresses and as students build reading stamina, the book selection process changes and becomes individualized according to their needs and desires. For example, a fluent reader would probably rather read a chapter book from cover to cover and then make another selection. The goal is to provide a structure that fosters the love of reading and provides the time necessary to become a fluent reader. Ideally, we want our students to be reading a variety of texts for 50 minutes daily. When they can do this, they have developed the attitude, skills, and habits necessary to become lifelong readers.

On Monday, we check each student's book selection. It doesn't take a great deal of time to do this, and it gives us a window into their understanding of book choice. Student responses shared during share circle is another way for us to collect evidence of their understanding of how to select books. Also, conferring with students during independent reading time gives us information about their ability to make wise book choices. When children are fairly competent with this skill, we begin meeting with small guided-reading groups, book clubs, and individuals in conferences. Children add their guided reading or book club texts to their book bags, which provides them with more text that fits into their just-right book category.

This piece of the puzzle may seem most out of reach for young children. But it can be done. It takes time, perseverance, and resources but is worth the effort. Children can choose books at an appropriate level and be freed from the leveled-book mania discussed in *Beyond Leveled Books*. Without choice, reading engagement rarely exists!

A students selects books for independent reading practice.

● ● ●

CHAPTER 3:
Teaching Reading Strategies

Building independent readers includes teaching reading strategies that help students become better readers each time they read. It isn't enough for us to have an organizational structure in place that supports independence; the organizational structure also has to have content. Explicit instruction in a few reading strategies taught well over time gives children the tools they need to engage in reading while they monitor their own learning. During the first six weeks of school, we teach our students to read using decoding strategies, while simultaneously helping them understand what they are reading by using the comprehension strategy of summary.

Students learn how to decode tricky words using fix-up strategies. There are three purposes for these strategies:

1. To provide readers with a range of strategies to figure out unfamiliar words independently
2. To build reading stamina by giving students a purpose for reading
3. To teach children how to monitor for meaning by cross-checking word choice

Having a variety of decoding strategies is foundational for independent reading. Being able to decode in order to make meaning and read fluently increases reading stamina.

Along with the decoding strategies, our reading instruction includes teaching comprehension strategies. We begin with summarizing narrative text because it teaches students how to understand and remember what they are reading. The ability to summarize offers concrete evidence that students can carry the important parts of a story in their heads. They are taught to check for understanding themselves by summarizing a story at different points along the way.

Narrative stories have characteristics and structures that knowledgeable readers use to understand text. Some children arrive at school with little experience with books, however, and they need instruction to understand the structure of narrative text. Young readers can make greater sense of text when they know how to use summarization effectively. Explicit teaching of summary appears to improve memory and recall of details, as well as the main ideas discussed in the text (Armbruster, Anderson, and Ostertag, 1987). Younger and less-successful readers, however, wait until the end of reading to summarize, which is not very effective (Paris, Wasik, & Turner, 1991). In our mini-lessons, we model how to summarize throughout reading for greater understanding.

The use of a story-grammar framework (setting, characters, problem, attempts at problem resolution, and resolution) is one of the most commonly researched instructional techniques. Children who are instructed in the elements of story grammar achieve higher levels of comprehension (Baumann & Bergeron, 1993; Davis, 1994). Therefore, we teach our students to use the elements of story grammar to summarize text.

Critical literacy evolves from identifying the elements of story grammar. From this starting point, readers can ask and answer *who, what, where, when, why,* and *how* questions to demonstrate their understanding of key details in a text. They can also describe how a character in a story responds to major events and challenges and use this insight to interpret the theme at a personal level. Readers learn to pay attention to their personal

Building Independent Readers © 2012 by Linda Lee & Mary Haymond • Scholastic Teaching Resources

responses to the characters, the problems the characters encounter, and how the setting influences the characters' thinking. Thus, the ability to summarize narrative text lays the foundation for all the work on reading comprehension to come.

DECODING STRATEGIES

Teaching decoding strategies using gradual release of responsibility is a powerful way for students to learn to choose knowledgeably from a variety of strategies. They then cross-check to make sure the word sounds right, makes sense, and looks right. The student-share example shown below illustrates the power of this instruction.

In early October, the children were gathered on the carpet ready to share and reflect on their work during independent reading time. Four students explained how they used their fix-up strategies when they were reading their just-right books.

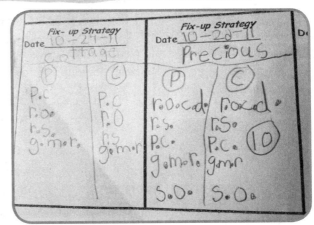

A student's fix-up strategies for *cottage* and *precious*

Jesse had marked three pages in his book with sticky notes. He turned to one page and shared his thoughts: "The word I didn't know was *information*. I predicted the word by using the parts of the word that I knew, like *in* and *for*. Then I confirmed it was the right word by reading on and it made sense."

It was Sarah's turn to tell about her tricky word. She quickly turned to a page in her book and said, "A word that I got stuck on was *cottage*. I knew the word *cot* and then I looked at the picture, and there was something that looked like a *cottage*, so I predicted *cottage* was the word. I confirmed it was the word by reading on and it made sense and sounded right. Without figuring out that word, I don't think I would have understood what was happening on the page."

Gavon was called on next. He had already turned to the page he wanted to share and said, "I came to this word *rhinoceros* and I tried to predict it using all my strategies . . . slide through the word, running start, chunks, and picture clues, but there weren't any pictures. So, I used another word. I kept on reading, and it made sense."

Brock was the last student to share: "I was stuck on the word *laces*. I figured it out by looking at the picture, and I saw a tennis shoe. Then I took a running start and got my mouth ready for the *L*, and the word just popped out of my mouth. I know the word I predicted is a keeper because I read the sentence again to be sure that it made sense and sounded right."

The ability to decode requires the use of the following three information systems:

✰ Phonics
✰ Grammar
✰ Meaning

From these information systems, we teach specific fix-up strategies so students can figure out unknown words independently.

▶Information Systems

Young children may not understand when they access phonics, but they know when "sound it out" works for them. Likewise, when students reread and think about whether the unknown word sounds right, they do not know they are using their knowledge of language patterns, word functions, or grammar. They may not recognize that their understanding comes from their background knowledge. However, the three information systems are the core of helping children develop concrete strategies to decode unknown words.

⬈ *Phonics and Word Analysis*

Phonics and word analysis use letter-sound relationships and patterns to predict and/or confirm words.

Predict:
- ✩ Get your mouth ready (first letter/blend/digraph).
- ✩ Point and slide to sound it out.
- ✩ Look for chunks and word families.
- ✩ Look for prefixes, suffixes, compound words, and word derivatives.

Confirm:
- ✩ Does it look right?
- ✩ Does it sound right?
- ✩ How do you know?

⬈ *Structure of Grammar*

Readers use their knowledge of language patterns and word functions to predict and confirm words.

Predict:
- ✩ Reread it (take a running start).
- ✩ What would sound right?
- ✩ What kind of a word do you need (noun, verb, adjective, and so on)?

Confirm:
- ✩ Does it sound right when you read it that way?
- ✩ How do you know?

⬈ *Meaning*

Meaning is accessed by melding knowledge of the world, information already gained from the text, and illustrations to predict and confirm words.

Predict:
- ✩ Stop and think about what's happening (what would make sense).
- ✩ Look at the pictures.
- ✩ Use what you know from life.
- ✩ Read on and come back to the word.
- ✩ Make a meaningful substitution.

Confirm:
- ✩ Does it make sense?
- ✩ How do you know?

▶Using All Three Systems

The goal is for readers to access all three information systems as they figure out unfamiliar words while reading independently. The following scenarios are examples of how we use specific prompts to help children integrate the use of the information systems to predict and confirm unknown words.

✮ A student usually predicts words using *phonics*, but does not pay attention to *meaning*. During guided reading and conferring, we help with understanding *meaning* by asking, "Does it make sense when you read it that way?" To promote *structure*, we ask, "Does it sound right when you read it that way?"

✮ Another student predicts words primarily using picture clues *(meaning)*. In guided reading and individual conferences, we help them use *phonics* by asking, "If you slid through the word, would the letters match?" To support *structure*, we ask, "Does it sound right when you read it that way?"

✮ Someone else may predict words using knowledge of sentence *structure*. Again, in small group and conferences, we foster the use of *phonics* by asking, "When you slide through the word, do the letters match?" For *meaning*, we ask, "Does it make sense when you read it that way?"

FIX-UP STRATEGIES

When we present the information systems to children, we call them fix-up strategies. Essentially, these strategies include any technique, principle, or rule that enables a reader to decode unknown words and gain meaning from text. We model the strategies listed below for our students during read-to and shared-reading mini-lessons.

I use strategies to predict and confirm tricky words.

✮ Stop and think what would make sense and sound right.

✮ Look at the picture and think about what would make sense.

✮ Reread and get your mouth ready to say the word.

✮ Point and slide to sound it out.

✮ Use chunks you know.

✮ Read on and then come back to the word.

✮ Use what you know from your life that makes sense.

✮ Ask someone.

✮ Always ask yourself:

Does it make sense?

Does it sound right?

Does it look right?

How do I know?

We begin teaching fix-up strategies during the first week of school or reviewing them with older students who are already familiar with the strategies. Before they can select just-right books, students will need to know how to use fix-up strategies to figure out unknown words. When most young children enter school, the only word-attack strategy they may know is "sound it out." Sounding out a word is an excellent reading strategy, but it isn't advisable to limit children to just one way of decoding. They come into our classrooms with different strengths, and our job is to capitalize on these strengths to help them find success as readers.

▶ Introducing the Fix-Up Strategies

We use two types of whole-group mini-lessons to teach fix-up strategies.

1. **Teach/Review:** The first type of lesson is designed to teach and/or review the strategies. We continue these lessons for approximately four weeks. On Monday, we do think-alouds and model the uses of two new strategies that we have written on a chart. We stage coming to unknown words in a book or an article, then we try each fix-up strategy on the chart. Next, we identify which strategy works better and explain why it worked with that particular word. Remember to plan accordingly. For the lesson to be successful, the words have to be decoded using one or the other of the strategies being modeled. After the lesson, we ask students to turn and talk about what they learned.

    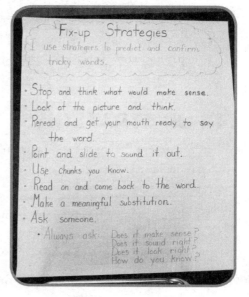

    Classroom chart of fix-up strategies

    Tuesday's lesson starts with an invitation for the class to become reading coaches. We ask students to identify the fix-up strategies they observed us using the day before. The lesson proceeds with children coaching us to use the fix-up strategies listed on the chart. We always ask students to explain why they selected one strategy over the other.

    This sequence continues until most of the reading strategies have been introduced. It takes about four weeks of instruction to model all the strategies listed on the chart (see list on page 29). It is difficult to give advice about which strategies should be introduced or reviewed first; that information depends on the grade level you teach. The pace of the lessons also varies according to how much students know about using fix-up strategies. If most students know how to use a variety of strategies, we move fix-up strategy instruction to guided-reading groups and/or individual conferences.

2. **Cross-Checking:** After all the fix-up strategies have been modeled, the mini-lessons change. At this point, many children are beginning to use these strategies when they come to a tricky word. Now the teaching is focused on how to cross-check when predicting and confirming tricky words. Cross-checking is what readers do when they use two or more sources of information to predict and confirm unknown words.

 Building Independent Readers © 2012 by Linda Lee & Mary Haymond • Scholastic Teaching Resources

How Many Ways of Knowing Game: We use a game called "How Many Ways of Knowing" to teach students how to cross-check. The directions for playing the game are very simple. Use sticky notes to cover about five words in the text. Select words that readers can figure out using the following strategies: "stop and think what would make sense" and "read on and then come back to the word." Project the text using a document camera or by another method. As you read the text and come to a covered word, ask a student to predict the word. Ideally, the student should identify the word, explain how he or she **predicted** it, and then share how he or she **confirmed** the prediction using as many strategies as possible. Write the word on a sticky note, and list all the strategies used to confirm the word choice. Below are examples of student responses.

"I predict the word is *castle*. I used the picture clues and thought about what would make sense. Then I reread the sentence with the word in it. It made sense and sounded right. I confirmed it was the word by reading on and it made sense again. I think I used three strategies."

"I predict the word is *bright*. I noticed that in this poem the last word in every other sentence ends in the '-ight' chunk. I reread the sentence using the word *bright*, and it made sense and sounded right. I confirmed it was the word by reading on, and it made sense and matched the rhyming pattern of the poem."

Always uncover the word and make a visual match between the student's prediction and the actual word. Discuss which parts of the word students could have used to help figure out the meaning if it had not been covered. You also want your students to predict words using their visual features; covering up the word, however, helps activate meaning and structure. Saving word analysis for the last strategy seems to help children focus on the visual features of the word. You should cover up basic sight words that you don't want them to sound out. If students are having a great deal of difficulty decoding a word, offer scaffolding by leaving its beginning letter or letters uncovered.

▶Assessment

We continue playing the How Many Ways of Knowing game for at least four weeks and stagger strategy review lessons throughout the year, based on the needs of our students. Depending on the reading levels and experiences of our students, the shared-reading mini-lessons sometimes extend longer at the beginning of the year. In general, though, collecting data from records of oral reading, conferences, and observations helps us determine when to move fix-up strategy instruction and practice to small-group and individual work.

We also teach students how to use sticky notes to collect evidence that they can use fix-up strategies to figure out a tricky word. When students come to share circle, they are prepared to explain how they solved a reading challenge. We collect notes to assess each student's ability to monitor for meaning when they read.

In order for independent reading time to be productive, children need to have a bank of fix-up strategies. Knowing what to do when they come to a tricky word fosters self-reliance. Students feel pride in their accomplishment and are willing to continue the work. The result is that students get better at reading each time they read. They are willing to put in the practice because they feel successful.

SUMMARIZING

As children are learning to use the fix-up strategies to decode words, it is important that they recognize that the real prize in learning to read is to get meaning, knowledge, and enjoyment from text. In order for students to use all the comprehension strategies effectively, they must be able to determine the important parts of a story. That is why we teach summarizing as their first comprehension strategy. It is the foundation upon which all other comprehension strategy work is based.

Summarizing is the ability to carry the important parts of a story in your head using the elements of story grammar. Young children often have difficulty summarizing text because they want to tell everything. They are generally more comfortable with retelling than summarizing. Retelling is defined as telling everything you can remember about the text. In contrast, the ability to summarize what's most important requires readers to ask essential questions, make inferences and predictions, create sensory images to arrive at the theme, and make meaningful connections. The ability to think deeply about the text hinges on determining what's most important to understand and remember.

We suggest that kindergartners spend most of the year orally retelling stories, acting out the text, and completing artistic responses using the elements of story grammar. In first grade, children would then be ready to review story grammar and use the elements to create their own summaries with pictures and words. By the end of second grade, most children would be capable of writing a summary.

▶ Story Grammar

At the beginning of the school year, our reading instruction includes teaching students how to understand and remember what they are reading by summarizing text. They learn to identify elements of story grammar including characters, setting, the character's goal, problem/solution, and sequence of events in a narrative text. Research identifies this as a common and necessary reading strategy (Allington, 2006). Children benefit from explicit instruction in text elements and the structure of stories. The ability to summarize text using the elements of story grammar is the first step in learning how to apply a comprehension strategy to understand and remember what is read.

Using the elements of story grammar gives readers the ability to make decisions about what to remember. Through instruction, readers learn to recognize how these text elements fit together to create the theme. They become aware of how the author is crafting the story to help convey the central message, lesson, or moral of the story.

Classroom Summary chart

 Building Independent Readers © 2012 by Linda Lee & Mary Haymond • Scholastic Teaching Resources

↗ *Using Story Maps*

Story maps provide an artistic approach to teaching our students how to summarize what they are reading—as they are reading. One of the first ways for readers to monitor for meaning as they read is to notice when they have lost track of story elements.

Story maps also help students summarize a story in an original way. A student's artistic interpretation of a story's meaning can reveal deep comprehension of characters, setting, problem, and solution. We have students work together to create a class mural that is a pictorial story map and then work individually to produce a story map that captures the key elements of story grammar.

A story map also provides a scaffold for communicating the summary of a story. After we demonstrate each step, children are ready to apply what they have learned. They create a story map for a just-right book they are reading during independent reading time. Emergent writers accomplish this task by labeling their drawings; more fluent writers add a sentence or two to their drawings.

▶Introducing Summarizing to Students

Summary lesson plans begin with orchestrating a read-to mini-lesson. As students listen and watch, we read aloud a story and model how to identify the elements of story grammar, emphasizing that these story elements are used to *determine what is important in the text,* and then using that information to create an oral summary of it.

After at least three read-to lessons, we implement the shared-reading teaching approach. With our guidance, students discuss what is important in the text and use the information to create a summary. We provide students with a variety of opportunities to summarize the text. For example, turn-and-talk with a partner is

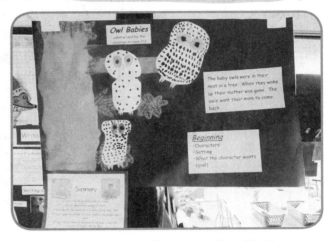

A story map for the beginning of *Owl Babies*

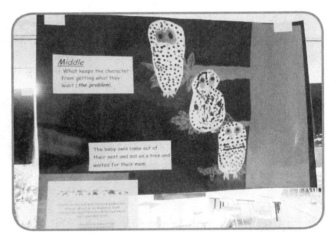

A story map for the middle of *Owl Babies*

A story map for the end of *Owl Babies*

designed to involve all children in the discussion. Each child is held accountable for using the elements of story grammar to determine what was important in the story and then use that information to provide a brief summary of the text with a partner. Students also work with us and in groups to create a story-map mural based on their shared-reading experience. At this point, they are not yet asked to use the elements of story grammar to understand and remember what they are reading independently. The goal here is to give them guided practice within a group. We display the story-map mural so it serves as a permanent chart for reading and writing a summary. Students refer to it often as they gain control of summarizing text independently.

A student's summary

After many demonstrations of oral summaries and completing the mural class project, we model how to create an individual story map to produce a summary. On the first day, we model how to select a just-right book and then read it for meaning in preparation for developing a story map. This may sound silly, but many children will attempt to create a story map for a story they cannot read or have not read. If many of your students are reading chapter books, we recommend that their choice be limited to short stories. Basal readers of all levels are a great resource; for example, our basal reading series is an anthology of wonderful short stories. Again, some students will need your support in finding narrative text that they can read. Once they have selected a just-right book, students are expected to read the book during independent reading time, and they may share their book choice at share circle. By the end of this process, most students can summarize what they have read.

Guide for Making a Story Map

Use this guide to create the story maps in Lessons 18–20 on page 100–103.

Beginning
- ✧ Write the title and the author's name.
- ✧ Draw the setting.
- ✧ Draw the character(s) and what is most important at the beginning of the story.
- ✧ Write about where the character(s) are and what they want.

Middle
- ✧ Draw how the character(s) are trying to reach their goal and a problem they encounter.
- ✧ Write about how the character(s) are trying to solve the problem so they can reach their goal.

End
- ✧ Draw how the story ends. How does the character(s) solve the problem(s)?
- ✧ Write about how the story ends. Do the character(s) reach their goal?

Building Independent Readers © 2012 by Linda Lee & Mary Haymond • Scholastic Teaching Resources

▶ Assessment

At this point, you need to determine if your students can summarize text. During share circle, ask them to summarize a just-right book. Rate their ability to do this using the Reading Comprehension Strategies Rubric: Summarizing Fiction sheet below. When most of your students can summarize what they are reading, move this work to small-group instruction.

Children need to view summarizing as a way to prove to themselves they can understand and remember the important parts of what they have read. Determining what is important in a text is the first step in monitoring for meaning while reading. All the other comprehension strategies depend upon a reader's ability to determine what is most important. Otherwise, the reader does not go below a surface understanding of the text. For example, children may retell all the events in *The Little Red Hen* instead of synthesizing the events into one big idea: "None of the Little Red Hen's friends will help her." We schedule our plans so that Mondays and Tuesdays always include a fix-up strategy mini-lesson until we have determined that most readers are using the decoding strategies

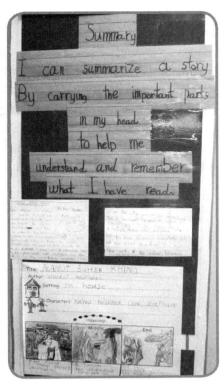

A Summary chart and student examples in the classroom

Reading Comprehension Strategies Rubric: Summarizing Fiction

Level 4	Level 3	Level 2	Level 1
Provides all elements of story grammar in logical sequence and with some extension to overall theme.	• Identifies important characters. • Identifies setting. • Describes what the character wants. • Describes what keeps the character from getting what he or she wants. • Tells how the problem gets solved. • Shares the resolution.	Some details in the summary show limited understanding of the story.	Little or no evidence of understanding the story.

independently. Children who still need support meet with us in guided-reading groups that are focused on decoding strategies. On Wednesdays, Thursdays, and Fridays, we teach summarizing comprehension lessons until most students are ready to use a summary to get to the theme of a story. (See the lesson-planning calendars on pages 54, 68, 78, 91, 105, and 116.)

By the middle of October, our students are able to sustain their independent reading for at least 50 uninterrupted minutes. This is possible because they make wise book choices, have developed a range of fix-up strategies, and can use the elements of story grammar to summarize what they have read.

Patterned/Predictable Books for Students to Summarize

The following patterned/predictable books are good options for students to read and summarize in writing.

Buzz Buzz Buzz by Byron Barton	*Across the Stream* by Mirra Ginsburg
A Dark, Dark Tale by Ruth Brown	*The Chick and the Duckling* by Mirra Ginsburg
Four Fur Feet by Margaret Wise Brown	*The Bus Stop* by Nancy Hellen
The Runaway Bunny by Margaret Wise Brown	*Where's Spot?* by Eric Hill
Mr. Gumpy's Outing by John Burningham	*Titch* by Pat Hutchins
Have You Seen My Cat? by Eric Carle	*The Carrot Seed* by Ruth Krauss
The Very Busy Spider by Eric Carle	*Just Me and My Puppy* by Mercer Mayer
The Very Hungry Caterpillar by Eric Carle	*The Cake That Mack Ate* by Rose Robart
The Very Quiet Cricket by Eric Carle	*Three Ducks Went Wandering* by Ron Roy
Are You My Mother? by P. D. Eastman	*Where the Wild Things Are* by Maurice Sendak
The Gingerbread Boy by Paul Galdone	*Have You Seen My Duckling?* by Nancy Tafuri
The Teeny Tiny Woman by Paul Galdone	*The Great Big Enormous Turnip* by Alexei Tolstoy
The Three Bears by Paul Galdone	*The Big Fat Worm* by Nancy Van Laan
The Three Billy Goats Gruff by Paul Galdone	*Cookie's Week* by Cindy Ward
The Three Pigs by Paul Galdone	*The Napping House* by Audrey Wood

• • •

 Building Independent Readers © 2012 by Linda Lee & Mary Haymond • Scholastic Teaching Resources

CHAPTER 4:
Creating a Climate for Learning

One of our goals for the first six weeks of school is to establish classroom routines that set the stage for productive learning. This begins on the very first day of school. When we build a strong sense of community, our children find it easier to take risks in many ways, including the self-selection of their own reading materials. They learn that everyone in the classroom is at a different place in his or her learning and that we are all responsible for supporting each other as we grow as readers.

POSITIVE RELATIONSHIPS

Establishing community in the classroom begins with the teacher. It is critical that we bond with each and every student. The children we teach need to receive the message that they are cared for and that we view each one as an important member of the classroom community. We strive to make a daily connection with each one, taking the time to learn about individual interests and to listen to concerns. When students know what we want them to do, they eagerly live up to these expectations. Therefore, we intentionally show them how to listen to one another and how to demonstrate respect through their actions and words. We immerse students in respectful, considerate speech. This modeling leads to the building of personal relationships that are the foundation to a successful community. We can spend a lot of energy telling children to be kind to each other, but the key to effective learning is modeling and practicing kind behavior instead. It's essential to acknowledge students' approximations when they exhibit thoughtful consideration toward others. "Catching" a child in the act of being a respectful community member is critical. In our community meetings during the first six weeks of school, we share the kind words and considerate behaviors relayed to us. This makes a lasting impression on the other students and helps us establish a caring community.

STAMINA

As we are building community, we teach our students what it means to have stamina. They need to understand this concept in order for them to become independent readers for 50 uninterrupted minutes a day. During the first few weeks of school, we read books about people who have accomplished great things as a result of their stamina. Some of these titles are used in the lesson plans in the next section of the book. We also use them for read-alouds at other times of the day. Here is a list of some of the books we recommend:

Wilma Unlimited: How Wilma Rudolph Became the World's Fastest Woman Runner by Kathleen Krull (Harcourt, 1996)
Wangari's Trees of Peace by Jeanette Winter (Harcourt, 2008)
Walk On! A Guide for Babies of All Ages by Marla Frazee (Harcourt, 2006)
The Librarian of Basra: A True Story From Iraq by Jeanette Winter (Harcourt, 2005)
Salt in His Shoes by Deloris Jordan & Roslyn M. Jordan (Simon & Schuster, 2000)
Wolf! by Becky Bloom (Scholastic, 1999)

Students quickly make the connection between stamina and the ability to accomplish one's goals.

This display celebrates students' independent reading successes.

ENVIRONMENT

In addition to book selection, we believe that children also need to have a choice in where they read in class. The room should feel like a warm and inviting learning environment to all who enter. We put a great deal of thought into arranging the physical space in our rooms. The space should foster independence and be designed for a variety of uses and student groupings. We begin by considering the best place for teaching whole-group mini-lessons, which require an open area for children to sit in and a chair for the teacher. An easel and other necessary supplies should be placed nearby.

 Building Independent Readers © 2012 by Linda Lee & Mary Haymond • Scholastic Teaching Resources

Open area for teaching whole-group mini-lessons

Reading nook

Areas for discussion

One way to encourage independence is by teaching children how to take care of their own needs. We live by the following motto: "Don't do anything for students that they can do for themselves." The different areas in our rooms and all supplies are clearly labeled, and we teach students routines for accessing and using them. We also consider traffic patterns so students can move about most efficiently during transitions and while they are working independently. We practice and review routines periodically to make sure that time is being used effectively.

Furniture is arranged to create nooks and crannies in which students can cozy up for reading. As with adults, children have different preferences for their favorite spots to read.

We have allocated places where partners can read and discuss their reading. The classroom also needs a location for a small-group instruction and student-run book clubs.

The proper lighting is important in classrooms. Our classroom is partially lighted with lamps to lessen the potentially harsh impact of overhead florescent lightening. There is a growing body of evidence of the negative effect that fluorescent lighting can have on individuals with emotional, behavioral, and/or psychological challenges.

MANAGEMENT

We do not use a complicated behavior management system in our classroom. We have found that classes are best managed by maintaining a quick, intentional pace with high energy and enthusiasm. Making the content relevant, interesting, and fun is critical for maintaining student focus. Actively involve the children with turn-and-talks, whiteboards that show their thinking, and group responses after a thinking pause. And throw in a little humor now and then to keep students on their toes and connected with you.

▶ Behavior Expectations

Few students need behavior plans, but those who do should have tailor-made plans for their specific needs. A plan should be developed with input and consensus from the student, parents, counselor, and classroom teacher. We think it's important to emphasize student strengths and positive outcomes rather than inappropriate behaviors. The plan should focus on changing student behaviors rather than punishment. Finding what motivates the child is essential as is the teaching of behaviors that take the place of those that are inappropriate. We have found that the other children don't mind such interventions, even if another student is getting more attention. Typically, they are well aware of the student's challenging behavior and are happy to see a classmate making progress. Everyone benefits from a calm, productive classroom.

▶ Responsibility Expectations

Our classrooms operate under the assumption that we are all learners and teachers. Therefore, we each have a responsibility not only to ourselves but also to the other members of our community. Our classroom members emphasize learning and letting others learn. The entire community is responsible for setting the expectations rather than the teacher exclusively.

At the beginning of the year, we spend four to six weeks mapping out ideas that will help us build the most successful learning environment. Each day, we discuss the behaviors that enabled us to achieve our best learning. As teachers, we explicitly model everything that we expect from one another. We clearly state that these are the expectations for our classroom and that when we are not living up to them, we are not able to achieve our best learning. When students act with responsibility, their learning is enhanced and their potential is increased.

Children will also learn best if they make attempts first and then seek help. They are encouraged to ask peers to help solve problems before asking the teacher. We teach our students to "ask three, then me" so that they ask three classmates for help before approaching us. We also specifically model how to be a "helper" and not a "fixer." When a child does seek assistance, peers should not supply answers or solutions because

Students understand classroom expectations for listening.

that doesn't help their classmate learn. Instead, helpers should provide a process for solving the problem that scaffolds the classmate to learn and solve the problem independently.

These high expectations reflect our belief that children are indeed capable of taking responsibility for their own learning. We trust their ability to be partners in setting and achieving their learning goals. The results of these high expectations often surpass even our own visions of what children are truly capable of accomplishing.

Another management tool we use is a list of listening expectations that defines teacher responsibilities for teaching and student responsibilities for learning. We begin each mini-lesson by reviewing this chart.

Building Independent Readers © 2012 by Linda Lee & Mary Haymond • Scholastic Teaching Resources

Listening Expectations

Teacher Responsibility: To teach so you can do good work quickly.

Student Responsibility: To watch and listen so you can use what is being taught.

You are sitting by your partner.

You are not engaged in side talk.

You are watching, listening, and thinking.

You are actively participating in all parts of the lesson.

▶ What's Helpful Chart

After experiencing independent reading for a few weeks, students gain a sense of what is helping them develop their reading stamina and what diminishes it. At this point, we ask them for input in creating a What's Helpful chart. It's important to let children determine the criteria. The chart below is an example created by our students last year. Each year, the chart looks a bit different, depending upon the input given by children.

What's Helpful	What's Not Helpful
Talking quietly about reading.	Being noisy.
Being left alone so you can think.	Bothering others.
Concentrating.	Not paying attention.
Making good book choices so you can be productive.	Up and down, to and fro.
Believing in yourself.	Not making good choices.
Staying in one spot.	Not believing in yourself.
Caring for others; we are all teachers.	Sitting by others.

LESSON PLANS

During the past ten years, we have field-tested the lesson plans on pages 54–125 in our classrooms. Teaching this sequence of lessons has allowed nearly all of our students to productively sustain independent reading for 50 minutes every day. Their amazing growth as reader is the result of being given the gift of time to practice. Be aware that the pace of the lessons will vary each year depending on the assessed needs of our students.

▶Pacing

The first time we embark on any journey, we tend to follow a road map. The second time, we head toward that destination, we develop our own route. When you use the lesson plans, adapt them to meet the needs of the students in your classroom.

First-grade teachers, for example, may need to teach the fix-up strategy lessons throughout the entire year. Book-choice lessons will often take longer because of the number of emergent readers in first grade. Independent reading time will be shorter because it takes time for six- and seven-year-olds to develop stamina. They may not be able to sustain with text for 50 minutes until January. First-graders may also need more opportunities to read predictable and patterned text to build a collection of just-right books for their book bags. You are a teacher-researcher and will know when to move on by using your assessment data including informal observations.

Second-grade teachers often move their fix-up strategy lessons to small-group instruction when most students can apply them independently. Pacing of the book-choice lessons is determined by teacher observation. After students can easily select just-right books, the lesson objective changes to setting authentic purposes for reading. The ultimate goal here is for students to develop a passion for reading.

Third-grade teachers spend less time reviewing book choice, fix-up strategies, and summarizing if their students have had this instruction. If students are not familiar with these concepts, the pacing will be similar to that of a second-grade class. More time may be needed to build community because students are increasingly aware of each other's reading levels. In third grade, oral-summary lessons can be replaced by those that teach written summaries. Again, pacing depends on evidence of student learning.

Although the pace of the lessons may vary, each of these three essential elements—book choice, fix-up strategies, and summarizing—must be taught in sequence for students to become independent readers. The lesson plans in this book give you a road map to follow as you begin the journey of building a productive independent reading program.

● ● ●

CHAPTER 5:
After the First Six Weeks

After the first six weeks, we use a variety of strategies to maintain engagement with our independent readers and to keep the workshop fresh.

✧ Each additional unit of study taught over the course of a year becomes increasingly complex and invigorates independent reading time. Children apply their new learning to fiction and nonfiction, which in turn influences the books they read.

✧ We teach students how to set goals for reading stamina and to record evidence in book logs. Additionally, as we confer with each child, we collaboratively set goals for reading improvement.

✧ As each new comprehension strategy is taught, we add writing in response to reading. This is designed to show children that readers do write about their reading.

✧ Because reading is a social process, children are given a variety of opportunities to partner-read and to talk about their reading with others.

✧ We continually model authentic purposes for reading and keep book choice as an evolving event.

✧ This entire process creates an atmosphere of learning that will positively affect children for life!

A YEAR-LONG PLAN FOR UNITS OF STUDY

The following year-long plan lists our units of study and reflects our current curriculum integrating the Common Core States Standards (CCSS). School districts across the nation are in the process of replacing their state standards with the standards developed by the Common Core Standards Initiative. To prepare for the change, we studied the new standards and found many commonalities with our current state standards.

The pacing of our units of study is driven by the formative and summative assessment data we collect about our children. The year-long plan provides a template for what and when we will teach each standard, but it is also flexible enough to accommodate the learning needs of all our students. We collect assessment data and use it intentionally to determine what our students know and can use as readers. We evaluate our teaching moves and spend more time with certain concepts, if necessary.

The type of genre used is not listed on our year-long plan because each comprehension strategy is taught using a balance of literature (fiction) and informational text (nonfiction).

Year-Long Plan: Units of Study

Unit of Study	Teaching Points With Common Core State Standards Integrated
September/October Fix-Up Strategies Summary (See lesson plans on pages 54–125.)	**Teaching Points:** ✿ Readers use phonics as a strategy to figure out unfamiliar words. They use letter-sound relationships or patterns of letters to predict and/or confirm what a word says. ✿ Readers use meaning as a strategy to figure out unknown words. They meld their knowledge of the world, of reading, and the information already gained from the text and illustrations to predict and/or confirm unknown words. ✿ Readers use grammar as a strategy to figure out unknown words. They use their knowledge of language patterns and word functions to predict and/or confirm unknown words in order to gain and maintain meaning. ✿ Readers use the elements of story grammar to provide a summary of what they have read. ✿ Readers describe the overall structure of a story, including a description of how the beginning introduces the story and the ending concludes the action. ✿ Readers use information from the illustrations and words in a print or digital text to demonstrate understanding of characters, setting, or plot.
November Theme (central message, lesson, or moral)	**Teaching Points:** ✿ Readers are aware of the way text elements fit together to create overall meaning (the theme). ✿ Readers use their knowledge of these elements to predict and synthesize as they build a sense of the theme. ✿ Readers recount stories, including fables and folktales from diverse cultures, and determine their central message, lesson, or moral. ✿ Readers can describe how characters in a story respond to major events and challenges.

   Building Independent Readers © 2012 by Linda Lee & Mary Haymond • Scholastic Teaching Resources

December/January	Teaching Points:
Background Knowledge/ Predictions	✧ Readers use what they already know to understand and remember what they have read.
	✧ Readers use what they already know to make predictions about a text. They read to confirm their hypothesis and continually adjust their predictions based on new information.
	✧ Readers interact with the elements of story grammar; they use their memories, personal experiences, and feelings to interpret the text in personal terms.
	✧ Readers distinguish between connections that are meaningful and relevant and those that aren't.
	✧ Readers compare and contrast the most important points presented by two texts on the same topic.
	✧ Readers compare and contrast two or more versions of the same story.
	✧ Readers acknowledge differences in the points of view of characters, including by speaking in a different voice for each character when reading dialogue aloud.
	✧ Readers describe the connection between a series of historical events, scientific ideas or concepts, or steps in technical procedures in a text.
February	**Teaching Points:**
Determining Importance	**Before Reading**
	✧ Readers question themselves to set a purpose for reading.
Main Idea and Details	✧ Readers skim the text to answer questions about who, when, and where, text type, and level of difficulty.
	✧ Readers scan text to determine how they will read it and how it is organized (table of contents, index, glossary, and so on).
	During Reading
	✧ Readers distinguish important from unimportant information depending upon their purpose for reading.
	✧ Readers use text structure and a variety of text features (headings, subheadings, labels, captions, diagrams, photographs, glossary, electronic menus, bold print, icons) to help them distinguish important from unimportant information.

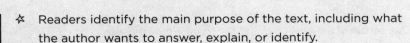

* Readers identify the main purpose of the text, including what the author wants to answer, explain, or identify.
* Readers identify the main topic of a multi-paragraph text as well as the focus of specific paragraphs within the text.

After Reading
* Readers question whether they have found the information they needed.
* Readers think to determine if they have any unanswered questions.
* Readers use their knowledge of important and relevant parts of the text to synthesize information for themselves and others.
* Readers determine how they will share what they have learned from their reading.

March/April
Asking Questions/
Inference

Teaching Points:
* Readers purposefully and spontaneously ask questions before, during, and after reading.
* Readers ask themselves questions when they read. Curious about the answers, they continue reading. Sometimes these questions are answered directly in the text and meaning is clarified. Clarifying questions are about who, what, when, and where.
* Readers ask questions that are not directly answered in the text. These are pondering questions; they ask how and why. Readers are forced to go beyond the text to find the answers. They make inferences.
* Readers determine the meaning of words or phrases in a text.

May/June
Sensory Images

Teaching Points:
* Readers create sensory images from their background knowledge/experience and the words in the text.
* Readers' sensory images are influenced by the images that others share.
* Readers' sensory images are fluid as they adapt them to incorporate new information.
* Readers describe how words and phrases (e.g., regular beats, alliteration, rhymes, repeated lines) supply rhythm and meaning in a story, poem, or song.

Building Independent Readers © 2012 by Linda Lee & Mary Haymond • Scholastic Teaching Resources

▶ Resources

We have included lessons for the first six weeks that are designed to help you build a classroom full of engaged, thoughtful readers (pages 54–125). What happens next depends on the learning outcomes set by your school district. The Common Core State Standards define in clear and consistent language the goals that students are expected to meet by the end of the school year. The standards allow teachers to determine how those goals should be met and what additional topics should be addressed.

There are many excellent resources that can help you develop lesson plans beyond the first six weeks. We have relied heavily on the professional books listed in the box below; they include units of study using literature and informational text.

Resources Designed to Build Your Knowledge Base About Best Practices

Mosaic of Thought: The Power of Comprehension Strategy Instruction
by Ellin Keene and Susan Zimmerman

What Really Matters for Struggling Readers: Designing Research-Based Programs
by Richard Allington

Resources That Provide Units of Study That Can Be Adapted to Classroom Use

Growing Readers: Units of Study in the Primary Classroom by Kathy Collins

Comprehension Connections: Bridges to Strategic Reading by Tanny McGregor

Reading With Meaning: Teaching Comprehension in the Primary Grades by Debbie Miller

Strategies That Work: Teaching Comprehension for Understanding and Engagement
by Stephanie Harvey and Anne Goudvis

The Primary Comprehension Toolkit: Language and Lessons for Active Literacy
by Stephanie Harvey and Anne Goudvis

GOAL SETTING

Student goals are an essential part of our reading instruction. They increase the value of the task. In the words of Schunk and Zimmerman, "Goals motivate students to exert extra effort and persistence, focus on relevant text features, and use strategies that will help them learn" (p. 18, 1996). These goals should be based upon what's been taught and individual learning needs. With guidance, students choose their own goals most of the time. We support each child in this endeavor during guided reading and conferring until everyone has succeeded and can do the task independently. To read effectively and stay engaged, students must have a goal for the reading activity.

Goals should be short-term, specific, attainable, and focused on understanding the text. Usually, the goals come from the comprehension strategy we are currently studying in the classroom. We listen to a child read aloud during a conference, and we ask questions. Then we offer a compliment for something the student has done well; this typically involves the progress toward reaching his or her goal. If the student has reached the goal, we celebrate and set a new goal. We model the new goal and then give the student time to practice with our support. Before we end the conference, we write the new goal or restate the old goal in the student's thinking journal. To ensure understanding of the goal, we ask the student to use his or her own words to verbalize the goal.

The goals we set collaboratively with our students come from the reading behaviors we observe during individual conferences and group work. Some of the more common goals can be organized into the following six groups:

Fluency

✫ *I will partner-read using my guided-reading book to build fluency.*

✫ *I will notice and use ending punctuation so I sound like a storyteller when I read.*

Fix-Up Strategies

✫ *I will listen to my reading voice. When it doesn't make sense or sound right, I will reread to find out what needs to be fixed.*

✫ *I will use the beginning and ending parts of words to figure them out.*

Book Choice

✫ *I will read the first three pages of a book to decide if it is just right for me.*

✫ *I will think about my purpose for reading before I select my books on Monday.*

Stamina

✫ *I will focus on my reading and ignore distractions.*

✫ *I will carefully select my books on Monday.*

Comprehension Strategies

✫ *I will write two questions at the end of each chapter. As I read the next chapter, I will pay attention to see if my questions have been answered.*

✫ *I will mark the places in the text that give me evidence to support my thinking about the theme.*

Vocabulary

✫ *I will stop and think about what the word could mean. I will read around the word and also check the illustrations to see if I can pick up clues about its meaning.*

✫ *If the word is in bold print, I will check the glossary to see what it means.*

BOOK LOGS

We have developed a book log specifically for students to record entries about just-right books. The purpose of the book log is to prove to children that every time they read a just-right book they can get better at reading. The log includes two rating categories: "easy" and "just right." When students read a just-right book, they record it in their log and rate its level of difficulty. The next time they read the book, their rating may have shifted to the "easy" category. Children are amazed that a book can become easy for them; they think the book has somehow changed. We have to point out that the book has remained the same, but they have grown as readers. Students who are reading a chapter book simply log each chapter as they finish it.

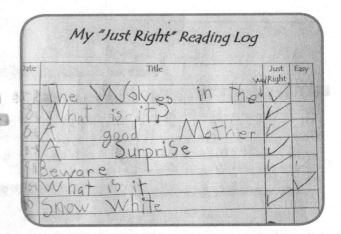

A completed book log for Just-Right books

WRITING ABOUT READING

Children in our classroom use a Thinking Journal–a folder with lined paper–created to collect written evidence that they are independently applying what has been taught. Each new unit of study requires the use of writing as a reflection tool. As children read, they write on sticky notes to explain how they figured out a tricky word. We limit their use to three notes per independent reading time. At the end of this period, students write one note about their smartest work and stick it in their Thinking Journal. Emergent readers seem to collect this type of evidence for most of the year. Other students rarely come to words they don't know so they drop this form of data collection fairly early. This is one option that children can use daily because it doesn't take much time away from actual reading.

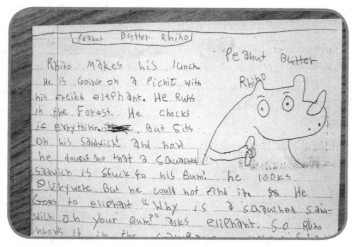

A page from a student's Thinking Journal

We reserve Thursdays for writing about reading. After using the gradual release of responsibility strategies to teach a new comprehension, we ask students to independently write about their reading. For example, during the book choice mini-lesson, students are asked to select a just-right book they would like to summarize. They read that book at least three times so they are ready to write a summary by Thursday.

Each new unit of study incorporates opportunities for children to write about their reading. We have found the following resource useful in designing activities that encourage children to write about their reading: *Writing About Reading: From Book Talk to Literary Essays, Grades 3–8* by Janet Angelillo.

PARTNER-READING

Our mini-lessons in September and October focus on teaching students how to talk about their reading, become reading coaches, and monitor for meaning using fix-up strategies and summary. Once these elements are in place, partner-reading provides the peer-learning approach to reading and complements the learning structures we have in place. We don't start partner-reading too soon because children's stamina needs to be developed during independent reading first. After most of the children display stamina as readers, our goal is to develop a classroom culture that fosters discussions about reading. To build purposeful talk about text, we establish daily partner-reading opportunities just before each share circle and again after

Students involved in partner-reading

guided reading groups. Students read with buddies throughout independent reading time on Fridays.

▶Buzzing About Books

At the beginning of share circle, children have approximately five minutes to talk with a partner about one of the books they are reading. This is critically important because share-circle time is limited and does not allow everyone to talk daily about reading. A re-analysis of the National Assessment of Educational Progress database found that social interaction was positively associated with increased reading activity (Guthrie, Schafer, Wang & Afflerbach, 1995). In particular, students of all ages who talked with friends about what they read were more active readers than students who engaged in less discourse about their literate behaviors.

After guided reading, we often pair children to reread their book. This helps builds fluency and confidence. Sharing the same book, one partner reads while the other serves as a reading coach. Usually their partner work focuses on using the fix-up strategies to figure out tricky words. It also helps build students' reading mileage. Working with a partner keeps the more reluctant reader engaged in the reading process and, along the way, helps build his or her reading stamina.

Children in book clubs also benefit from partner reading. The work of these pairs may focus on reading the book and talking about it in preparation for their next book club discussion. These partnerships are flexible and change throughout the school year as the needs and abilities of the students change.

Partner-reading in preparation for book club

On Fridays, we have children partner-read throughout the entire independent reading time. It gives them a new purpose for rereading and discussing the just-right books from their book bags. Partnerships provide students with opportunities to use the conversational moves they learned during the mini-lessons. They never seem to run out of things to talk about when sharing a book with a partner. Their talk can include a variety of interchanges, including the following:

- ✫ Sharing new knowledge
- ✫ Expressing an emotional response they had to a book
- ✫ Coaching each other to figure out tricky words
- ✫ Recommending books to each other
- ✫ Taking on the characters' voices as they read
- ✫ Sharing what they wrote in their thinking journals
- ✫ Explaining places they marked with sticky notes
- ✫ Elaborating on interesting characters and events from their books

Be sure to intentionally model each of these interchanges to help students build and expand their repertoires.

▶Management Strategies

When partners read to each other, they have a variety of options from which they can choose. They may decide to echo read, take turns reading pages, or choral read. We present the choices and then let partners decide which option will work for them. The most important element in partnerships is effective coaching, so we teach children how to coach each other including when to simply supply the tricky word to the partner. This occurs through our modeling and student practice during the fix-up strategies mini-lessons.

Children are partnered in different ways. We generally pair students who are reading at, or near, the same level. Pairing is usually done after a guided-reading group or a book club. When children know how to gracefully accept a partnership offer, they choose partners on Friday. We also manage choice of partnership by suggesting topical interests, for example, "John read a book about snakes. Who is interested in reading with John today?"

Five minutes before share circle, children meet with their partner. Because students always sit by their partner on the carpet, the sharing happens immediately. Once the signal is given, they know to gather their books, find their partner, and quickly sit side-by-side so they can begin sharing with each other.

KEEPING BOOK-CHOICE LESSONS INTERESTING

At the beginning of the school year, we spend two days a week teaching book choice. After the six to eight weeks it takes to teach how to choose books in each category, we continue to teach a book-choice lesson every Monday for the rest of the year. This lesson sets the tone for the week. In it, we share our lives as readers and ensure our lessons reflect what we actually do as readers outside of school. We discuss when and where we read, how we choose books, what type of books we prefer, and why we like them. The Monday book-choice lessons provide time to introduce different genres, purposes for reading, and series books.

Over time, we create a chart that reflects what has been taught during book-choice lessons. The sample chart below shows all the ways that readers choose books. At the beginning of Monday's book-choice lessons, we use the chart to activate prior knowledge about the many ways readers select books.

How to Make a Wise Book Choice

- ✯ Interesting front covers
- ✯ Blurb on the back of the book
- ✯ Recommendations made by others
- ✯ Answer a question
- ✯ Learn something new
- ✯ Connect to the characters, events
- ✯ Favorite authors
- ✯ Award-winning books
- ✯ Interest in the topic
- ✯ Reread old favorites
- ✯ New books

CONCLUSION

Over lunch, Mary and I sat down for a chat about how the morning had gone. Mary asked, "What was all the clapping about in your room at share circle?" I couldn't wait to tell her the story. We were in the third week of a unit of study on making connections. As of yet, no one in my classroom had transferred the thinking strategy to independent use. Mary had advised me to be patient and to not give up. I shared what had happened:

You were so right about being patient! As I began share circle this morning, I took a quick glance at my share circle list. It held some promise because my most vocal students were in line for sharing. As I invited students to share, they were able to summarize what they had read (proving they could hold the story in their head), identify the theme with supporting evidence from the text, or describe how they used a fix-up strategy to figure out a tricky word. I tried hard not to show my discouragement that no one had made a connection.

We were almost out of time, so I asked if anyone had made a connection. As I scanned the group, I was desperate to hear from someone who would offer a gem that would get other readers to think about their own connection to the text. Olivia, my most emergent reader, was the only one to raise her hand. My heart sank. Now that she had gained confidence with her ability to figure out tricky words, I thought that would be the content of what she wanted to share. I scanned the circle but couldn't ignore Olivia. She was up on her knees, waving her hand wildly in the air, seeking approval with her dark brown eyes. How could I resist? I invited Olivia to share. Just as I expected, she took a deep breath and proudly explained that she didn't have to use any fix-up strategies on her just-right book because she knew all the words. This was a touchstone moment for her, and I had to smile. Then she gave a summary of the eight-page text. The cleverly written decodable text was about a cat that didn't want to share her mat. After Olivia finished summarizing the story, I thanked her for sharing and was getting ready to dismiss the children for lunch when she threw up her little hand, palm out, and said, "Wait, there is more." She flipped to a page she had marked in the book with a sticky note. She read the one word of text on the page, "Spptttt." Olivia continued, "This is where the cat hisses at the other animals to get them off her mat. I made a connection to this part because it reminds me of my

brother Jayden. He never wants to share with me, and when I try to play with one of his toys, he yells at me and makes me give it back, just like the cat was yelling at the other animals so she could get her mat back. I know how it feels to want something and to be yelled at so you have to give it back. It hurts my feelings, and I bet it made the animals sad, too. My connection helped me learn to always share with other people."

I sat there stunned. Olivia nailed it! She not only made a connection to a line in the text with an experience from her life, but she also explained how the connection helped her think about what she could do to become a better person. The look on my face must have expressed my amazement because the entire class erupted in applause.

As we walked down the hall to gather the students from recess, we talked about all the Olivias we have taught over the years and what they have taught us. Children's capacity for thinking is nearly limitless if we create the learning conditions to support it (Ellin Keene, 2008). We are consistently reminded of how children can learn to lead intellectually powerful lives when they are given the gift of extensive time to practice reading, the choice of what to read, and the reading strategies to support them so they become life-long readers.

Our goal here is to help you create the conditions necessary to foster engaged and passionate readers. With this book, we have sought to detail each of the necessary components and then fit the pieces of the puzzle together to make independent reading possible for early readers in all classrooms, including yours.

● ● ●

Lesson Plans

Calendar for Lesson Plans
——— WEEK 1 ———

LESSON 1

Part 1, Book Choice: Introduce easy books and their purpose.

Part 2, Fix-Up Strategies: Introduce or review fix-up strategies.

LESSON 2

Part 1, Book Choice: Review easy books and their purpose.

Part 2, Fix-Up Strategies: Review the following strategies: stop and think
what would make sense; use picture clues; reread and
get your mouth ready.

LESSON 3

Summary: Introduce important elements at beginning of story:
characters, setting, and what characters want.

LESSON 4

Summary: Introduce important elements in middle of story: what's
keeping the character(s) from reaching a goal (the problem).

LESSON 5

Summary: Introduce important elements at end of story: how the
character(s) solved the problem (solution).

Building Independent Readers © 2012 by Linda Lee & Mary Haymond • Scholastic Teaching Resources

Lesson 1, Part 1

Book Choice

Teaching Point: The purpose of reading easy books is to build fluency, make meaning, and have fun.

Weekly Conversation Skill Focus: Body language

Materials:
- a short text for modeling fluent reading and making meaning
- chart paper and marker
- a variety of leveled books
- bubbles and blower (optional)

Preparation:
- Create the Easy Books chart shown below.
- Allot 10–15 minutes for students to read independently.

> ### Easy Books
> You read easy books to build fluency and make meaning.
> A book is easy if . . .
> ✯ you can read all the words.
> ✯ you sound like a storyteller.

 Activate Prior Knowledge

Display the Easy Books chart and read it to children. Then explain the purpose of the lesson, for example:

Today, we are going to learn about reading easy books. A book is easy for you if you can read all the words without any problems. It is easy for you if you sound like a storyteller when you read it. We call this fluent reading or fluency. As you learn more words, more books will be easy for you to read. Reading easy books is important because they help us warm up our reading muscles and become better readers. You will be reading easy books every day at the beginning of independent reading time, so it is important that you know how to pick an easy book. What is easy will be different for every one of you, so you need to know how to pick a book that's easy for YOU! Finally, reading easy books is fun!

Some of the terms on the Easy Books chart may be unfamiliar to students, but they will learn them over time. And remember, you should only expect students to approximate reading easy books during the independent portion of this first lesson.

 Model the Lesson

Display the front cover of the book you will be reading aloud. Read the title and author's name before you model the lesson.

Now I am going to read you a book that is easy for me. (Read book aloud with fluency and expression.) *This is an easy book for me because I could read all the words, and I didn't sound anything like a robot. I sounded just like a storyteller. What a great story! It was a fun book to read to you.*

 ## Focus the Conversation

Invite students to share what they have learned about easy books by talking with a partner. This will introduce body language, the most basic listening skill:

Talking about our reading and learning is a great way to help us remember ideas. Today I would like each of you to turn to the person next to you and use him or her as your listening partner. Sit with your knees touching each other, and look directly into your partner's face. It is polite to look people in the eye when you are having a conversation; it shows you are really paying attention to them. Okay, now I would like one partner to tell the other what makes a book easy. Then, I want the other partner to tell why we should read easy books.

Listen in on conversations, offering support as necessary. When there is a lull in the conversations, give a signal for children to stop and to return to a listening position. We have found that slowly counting backwards: "5, 4, 3, 2, 1—talking is done" is an effective way to call students back together, and it gives them a few seconds to wrap up their conversations. Ask two sets of partners who displayed appropriate body language to stand in front of the group. Describe what you saw them do with their bodies:

I heard and saw so much good talking and listening going on! I appreciate how Olivia stayed knee-to-knee with Isabelle. I also noticed that Micah looked Chase in the eyes during their whole conversation.

Celebrate students' good work by blowing bubbles on them.

 ## Restate the Teaching Point

Restate the teaching point by saying something like the following:

Remember, a book is easy for you if you can read all the words without any problem. You also sound like a storyteller as you read. So it's really the words that make a book easy for a reader, and as you learn more words, more books will be easy for you to read. Reading easy books is important because they help us warm up our reading muscles and become better readers.

 ## Move to Independent Practice

You can make book choice less overwhelming for students by providing several tubs of leveled books for children to choose from or by limiting how much of your classroom library they can access. We set out four tubs, and each tub contains a range of leveled books. For example, a tub with an orange dot contains levels A, B, C books; a tub with a yellow dot contains levels D and E books; a tub with a green dot contains levels G and H books; and a tub with a red dot contains levels I and J books. We tell children that the orange-dot books are the easiest, the yellow-dot books are a little hard, the green-dot books are even harder, and the red-dot books are the hardest to read, so they need to think carefully about where they might find easy books before beginning their search. Then we send children on their search:

Now it is time for you to choose some easy books. You may look through the tubs and choose two books that are easy for you to read. If you are not sure if they will be easy for you, you can ask me for help. When you have chosen your books, sit at your table and read them until I turn on the music. That will be your signal to come to the carpet.

Release a few children at a time to search for two easy books.

INDEPENDENT READING TIME

This will be a shortened version of independent reading time (about 10–15 minutes). Watch your students and make note of those who are having difficulty finding an easy book. During your next book-choice lesson, invite those students to stay with you and provide familiar patterned books for them to read. When children seem restless, stop the workshop, and turn on music to ready everyone for share circle. Do not expect all your children to have control over easy-book choice in just one lesson. As you continue to teach the easy-book choice lessons, students will become more proficient at choosing books.

SHARE CIRCLE

Gather students in a large circle in the meeting area. Celebrate students who found easy books and stayed engaged by describing what you saw them do:

I hope you all enjoyed looking for easy books. I noticed Jake looking at the covers and reading the first few pages of books. If he had trouble with a word, he put the book right back in the tub. I saw Maria flip through books and stop at a page in the middle to read. If she had trouble with even one word, she put the book back and selected another. Ruby, Josh, Zach, and Patty all found two books, sat down, and read them quietly. Anthony and Maria finished reading their easy books so they reread them. That is how we warm up our reading muscles and build fluency and stamina.

At this point in the week, share circle is brief and does not require too much sitting. Once you have acknowledged students' success with book choice, transition to the second part of the readers' workshop mini-lesson on fix-up strategies. The transition to the next lesson is seamless because children had the opportunity to move around when they were searching for their easy books.

For the next few weeks at the end of each day, we read a book that will become available for easy-book choice. We select books that we know are old favorites from previous school years, such as *Chicka Chicka Boom Boom* by Bill Martin, Jr. If you need guidance, ask other teachers which books they would recommend.

Lesson 1, Part 2

Fix-Up Strategies

Teaching Point: Readers use the following fix-up strategies to predict tricky words:

- Stop and think about what would make sense.

- Look at the picture and think.

- Reread and get your mouth ready to say the word.

Weekly Conversation Skill Focus: Body language

Materials:
- big book or text with strong picture support

- chart paper and marker

Preparation: • Create the Fix-Up Strategies chart shown below. Leave space at the bottom to
add more strategies as you teach them.
 • Select six words in the big book or picture book to use to model the fix-up
strategies. Make sure there are picture clues to support each word.

Fix-Up Strategies

You use these fix-up strategies to predict and confirm tricky words.

✫ Stop and think about what would make sense.

✫ Look at the picture and think about what would make sense.

✫ Reread and get your mouth ready to say the word.

 ## Set the Purpose

Explain the purpose of the lesson to students:

Not all books are easy books and, to grow as readers, we need to learn how to read challenging books, too. In those books, you will come across words you do not know. You need to have ways of figuring out tricky words so you can keep reading. I am going to teach (or review) you some fix-up strategies that will help you tackle tricky words.

Display and read the Fix-Up Strategies chart. Describe what the strategies are and how to use each strategy to figure out tricky words.

When you come across a word that you do not know, always think about what would make sense. Stop and ask yourself: "What would make sense?" All reading has to make sense, so that should be the first question you ask yourselves. As you think about what would make sense, one strategy you can use is to look at the pictures. Often pictures give us a clue about what the word might be and, if it makes sense in the sentence, there is a good chance that is the right word. Let me show you what I mean. (Demonstrate looking at the pictures in the book you are going to read. Really study the picture and talk about what you see.) *Another thing you can do when you are thinking about a word you do not know is to look at the first letter of the word. Then go back to the beginning of the sentence and reread, getting your mouth ready to say the word by making the first letter sound. You will be surprised how this strategy can help you figure out a word. Let me show you what I mean.* (Show this strategy using the same book.)

 ## Model the Lesson

Read a section of the book and model how you use each strategy to figure out a tricky word:

Okay, let's see how these strategies work when we are reading a book. I am going to read aloud from Dragon Tales *by Dav Pilkey, and when I come across a tricky word, I am going to look at the pictures and think what would make sense. Then I am going to go back to the beginning of the sentence to reread, getting my mouth ready to say the word by making the first letter sound.*

(Read the book aloud, pausing when you come to your first tricky word.) *Hmm . . . I can't read this word. I am not sure what it is. I am going to look at the picture and see if that helps me. I see a cat sitting in the snow. It looks so cold. Now I am going to read the sentence again and get my mouth ready for the tricky word. The word* cold *just popped out of my mouth. It makes sense, sounds right, and starts with the letter* c. *Okay, now I am ready to keep reading.*

Read along until you come to the next tricky word, and think aloud about how you solve it by using the strategies you introduced. Repeat this modeling for all the words you selected.

 ## Focus the Conversation

When your demonstration is finished, invite students to go knee-to-knee, eye-to-eye with a partner and name the fix-up strategies you used.

Readers, you watched me solve some tricky words today. You can use these fix-up strategies in your own reading, too. Turn to your partner and sit knee-to-knee and eye-to-eye, as we did earlier. Now, take turns telling each other which strategies I used to solve a tricky word. First partner, you tell one word and describe the fix-up strategy I used. Second partner, you take a turn telling another word and describing what I did. Continue until talk time is over.

Allow about 5 minutes for the partner discussion. As students talk, observe who is working well together and offer assistance to those who need it. When conversations are winding down (or getting off track), use a signal to call students back to the front. Compliment partners who actually went knee-to-knee and made eye contact. Ask a few students to share what their partner said.

 ## Restate the Teaching Point

Excellent work readers! Today, you learned three fix-up strategies you can use when you come across a word you do not know. You always stop and think what would make sense. Then you can check the pictures. You can also look at the first letter of the word and get your mouth ready to say it. I will be adding even more strategies to our Fix-Up Strategies chart as you learn them. You can always check the chart to remind yourselves which fix-up strategies you can use.

Lesson 2, Part 1

Book Choice

Teaching Point: The purpose of reading easy books is to build fluency, make meaning, and have fun.

Weekly Conversation Skill Focus: Body language

Materials:
- Easy Books chart from Lesson 1 (page 55)

Preparation:
- Choose an easy text and one that is slightly more difficult.
- Allot 10–15 minutes for students to read independently.

Activate Prior Knowledge

Ask students to explain what makes a book easy for a reader and why we read easy books. Have the Easy Books chart nearby for students to refer to and review it as necessary.

 ## Model the Lesson

In this lesson, students begin to share some of the responsibility for identifying easy books. Set up the situation for them:

I am going to read two books to you today. I am not sure if both of these books are easy for me. Watch and listen to me carefully. Decide whether both books are easy for me.

Model fluently reading the easy book. Then as you read the slightly more difficult book, model reading that sounds robotic and stumble over or stop at some words.

 ## Focus the Conversation

After the reading, ask partners to go knee-to-knee, eye-to-eye, and discuss whether the books were easy for you. Have a few partners share how they knew whether each book was easy. Continue reinforcing the behaviors you expect to see by highlighting partners who actually exhibited the body language necessary to having a conversation:

Readers, today and every day, you will know when a book is easy for you because you don't get stuck on tricky words, you sound like a storyteller, and you enjoy reading the book.

 ## Move to Independent Practice

Continue making a variety of leveled books available and open up another section of your classroom library. Have students choose two easy books from your classroom collection and then take them to their desk or table to read. If students finish both books, tell them to find two more easy books to read.

INDEPENDENT READING TIME

When almost everyone is settled, invite students who had difficulty finding easy books the day before to meet with you. Read several familiar patterned books and then offer these books to the children so they can read them at their desk or table.

As you circulate around the classroom, look for children who are meeting expectations, so you can highlight their work during share circle. Again, this is a shortened version of independent reading time (10–15 minutes), so watch students' levels of engagement, and when they begin to get restless, stop independent reading and gather for share circle. Ask children to bring one easy book to share.

SHARE CIRCLE

Focus on two students who met your expectations by describing what you saw them do. Ask pre-selected volunteers to read a few pages of their easy book. Tell the other children to listen to see if each book met the criteria listed on the Easy Books chart.

Building Independent Readers © 2012 by Linda Lee & Mary Haymond • Scholastic Teaching Resources

Lesson 2, Part 2

Fix-Up Strategies

Teaching Point: Readers use fix-up strategies to predict tricky words.

Weekly Conversation Skill Focus: Body language

Materials:
- big book or continuous text displayed via overhead projector, document camera, or another device
- sticky notes
- Fix-Up Strategies chart

Preparation:
- Select five words in the text to use to model the fix-up strategies. Cover each word with a sticky note so only its first letter(s) is visible.

Activate Prior Knowledge

Display and review the Fix-Up Strategies chart:

Remember, we are learning (or reviewing) fix-up strategies so that you will be able to figure out tricky words when you read. Knowing how to use fix-up strategies will give you strong reading muscles in your head so you will be able to figure out the tricky words.

Model the Lesson

Display the text you are going to read aloud. Ask students to be your reading coaches as you read. When you come to a tricky word, they can help you by suggesting one of the strategies on the Fix-Up chart.

Even if this is a review for your students, they will benefit from watching your actions during the think-aloud. It will help embed the language of the strategies so everyone's conversation is consistent.

Read a few pages of the text and stop at each partially covered word. Since only the first letter or letters are revealed, children have to suggest the following strategies: think what would make sense, then look at the picture, and reread and get your mouth ready:

I'm stuck on this word. Could someone be my reading coach? Thank you, Jenna, that's a good suggestion. I will try looking at the picture and thinking about what would make sense. I see a farm with lots of animals scattered around the yard, but this picture isn't helping me figure out the tricky word. Is there another strategy listed on the chart that might work? Thank you. Now I will try thinking about what would make sense, and then reread and get my mouth ready to say the word. It worked! The word barn *just seemed to pop out of my mouth. You taught me that if one strategy doesn't work, I should try another!*

Focus the Conversation

Ask partners to turn and talk about what they learned from coaching you. Focus the conversation by asking them to share how they decided which strategy to suggest. As partners are talking, listen for conversations that you can use to further the learning, and ask those pairs to share their thinking with the whole group. Then point out students who went knee-to-knee, made eye contact, and stayed tuned in to each other.

Restate the Teaching Point

Thank students for coaching you so effectively and summarize the lesson:

Instead of just telling me what each word was, you gave me fix-up strategies to try. To help me figure out tricky words, I can ask myself what would make sense, look at the pictures, and reread and get my mouth ready.

Lesson 3

Summary

Teaching Point: To understand and summarize a story, readers identify the important elements at its beginning: characters, setting, and what the characters want (goals).

Weekly Conversation Skill Focus: Body language

Materials:
- fiction
- chart paper and marker
- Easy Books chart

Preparation:
- Select a fiction title you read earlier in the week. (We suggest a title such as *The Three Billy Goats Gruff* by Paul Galdone.)
- Create the Summarize chart shown below.
- Create the Speaking and Listening chart shown in the Share Circle on p. 64.
- Allot 10–15 minutes for students to read independently.

Summarize

You can summarize a story by carrying the most important parts in your head. This will help you understand and remember what you read.

Here are the important parts of a story:

✫ **Beginning** Characters
 Setting
 Goal: what the characters want

✫ **Middle** Problem: what keeps the characters from getting what they want

✫ **Ending** Solution: characters get what they want

Activate Prior Knowledge

Display the Summarize chart and read it to children:

Today, I am going to read you a story and identify what's important to remember at the beginning: the characters, the setting, and the goal, or what the characters want. Remembering these elements will help you understand what the story is about. This is called summarizing a story. I want you to watch and listen to me while I read the story. Pay close attention to how I think about the characters, the setting, and what the characters want.

 ## Model the Lesson

Introduce the book you are going to read and remind children that you read it to them earlier in the week, too:

I am going to read The Three Billy Goats Gruff *and will stop when I think the beginning of the story has been introduced. Think about the most important parts in the beginning of the story: characters, setting, and goals.*

Read the text and think aloud to show when you know who the most important characters are, the setting of the story, and what the characters want. Then use this information to summarize the beginning of the story.

So in the beginning of this story, there are three goats. The goats live on a hill, but the grass there has been eaten. They are very hungry. They see fresh green grass on the other side of a bridge. They want to cross the bridge so they can get something to eat. Okay, now let's look at the Summary chart and see if I understood the beginning of the story.

 ## Focus the Conversation

Ask students to go knee-to-knee, eye-to-eye, and share what you included when you summarized the beginning of the story. Celebrate students who used body language appropriate for talking to a partner.

 ## Restate the Teaching Point

Review summarizing and the elements that make up the beginning of a story:

Today, you learned how to check your understanding of the beginning of a story. You need to remember the characters, the setting, and what the characters want when you summarize a story.

 ## Move to Independent Practice

Display and review the Easy Books chart. Remind children that once they have selected their two easy books, they need to sit at their tables and read. If they finish reading their easy books, they are free to select two more easy books. This will continue until it is time for share circle.

INDEPENDENT READING TIME

Continue to work with small groups and individuals to support their approximations with book choice. For your emergent readers, select several A through E leveled books because these books tend to be short, eight-page pattern books, and you can read several of them in 10 minutes. Then let children select one of these books to read on their own. Also encourage the rereading of familiar patterned texts they selected in previous lessons. This still leaves time for you to circulate around the room to provide encouragement as needed. Look for engaged students you can celebrate during share circle. When you decide it is time for share circle, ask children to bring one easy book with them to share.

SHARE CIRCLE

Start share circle by celebrating students who stayed engaged during independent reading time and found easy books to read. Ask volunteers to read a few pages of an easy book. Have other children listen to see if each book met the criteria listed on the Easy Books chart.

Note: We wait until Lesson 3 to introduce the protocol for share circle. We do most of the sharing during the first two lessons. This is the first time that children are invited to share their good work. Go over the rules on the Speaking and Listening chart with students to introduce the key components of listening, thinking, teaching, and learning during share circle. Eye contact between the speaker and the rest of the class is important. Make sure that when students are speaking, they are not directing their attention just to you. Everyone is a teacher and learner in the classroom, so set the foundation now.

> ### Speaking and Listening
> ☆ The speaker stands up.
> ☆ Listeners have their eyes on the speaker. Their books are closed.

Lesson 4

Summary

Teaching Point: To understand and summarize a story, readers identify the important elements in its middle: the problem.

Weekly Conversation Skill Focus: Body language

Building Independent Readers © 2012 by Linda Lee & Mary Haymond • Scholastic Teaching Resources

Materials:	• text used in Lesson 3
	• Summary chart
	• Easy Books chart
	• Speaking and Listening chart
Preparation:	• Allot 10–15 minutes for students to read independently.

 ## Activate Prior Knowledge

Display the Summary chart and read it to children. Then focus their attention on the part of the chart that explains the middle of a story:

Today, I am going to reread yesterday's story and identify what's important to remember in the middle: the problem—what's keeping the character from reaching his or her goal. Understanding this element helps you understand what the story is about. Remember, we call this summarizing a story. I want you to watch and listen to me while I read the story. Pay close attention to how I think about what keeps these characters from getting what they want. This is also called the problem of the story.

 ## Model the Lesson

Read the text and, through a think-aloud, uncover the most important information in the middle of the story. Describe when you know what the problem is. Then use the information to summarize the middle of the story.

The problem is that the goats want to cross the bridge to get some grass to eat, but a mean troll won't let them cross. If the goats try, the troll will eat them! Two of the goats convince the troll to spare them by waiting for the next goat to cross. The troll agrees, and the first two goats make it safely to the other side. Then the big billy goat tries to cross the bridge.

Stop reading before the problem is resolved.

 ## Focus the Conversation

Ask students to go knee-to-knee, eye-to-eye, and share what you included when you summarized the middle of the story. Celebrate students who used body language appropriate for talking to a partner.

 ## Restate the Teaching Point

Review summarizing and the elements that make up the middle of a story:

Today, you learned how to continue to check for understanding by summarizing at different points in the story. The lesson today focused on the middle of the story. Knowing the problems the character encounters helps you understand the story.

Moving to Independent Practice

Display and review the Easy Books chart. Remind children that once they have selected their easy books, they need to sit at their tables and read. If they finish reading their easy books, they are free to select two more easy books. This will continue until it is time for share circle.

INDEPENDENT READING TIME

Continue to work with small groups and individuals and support their approximations with book choice. This is a time when we get to know our students as readers and suggest other books in the room that would be easy. We have baskets organized by authors who write for the young reader. David Shannon's series of David books and Mo Willems' Piggy and Gerald series are good examples of high-interest, successful easy readers. They are a magnet for children.

Continue working the room, providing assistance and encouragement when needed. Also look for students whom you can highlight for engagement. When you decide it is time for share circle, ask children to bring one easy book to share.

SHARE CIRCLE

Before sharing begins, read and review the Speaking and Listening chart. Start share circle by celebrating students who stayed engaged during independent reading time and found easy books to read. Ask volunteers to read a few pages of an easy book. Have the other children listen to see if each book met the criteria listed on the Easy Books chart.

Lesson 5

Summary

Teaching Point: To understand and summarize a story, readers identify the important elements at its end: the solution.

Weekly Conversation Skill Focus: Body language

Materials:
- text used in Lessons 3–4
- Summary chart
- Easy Books chart
- Speaking and Listening chart

Preparation:
- Allot 10–15 minutes for students to read independently.

Activate Prior Knowledge

Display the Summary chart and read it to children. Then focus their attention on the part of the chart that explains the end of a story:

Today, I am going to continue to read The Three Billy Goats Gruff *and identify what's important to remember at the end of a story—the solution, or how the character solves the problem. Remembering this element will help you understand what the story is about. I want you to watch and listen to me while I read the story. Pay close attention to how I think about the way the story ends.*

 ## Model the Lesson

Read the text and, through a think-aloud, uncover the most important information at the end of the story. Describe when you know how the characters get what they want. Then summarize the end of the story:

At the end of the story, the big billy goat solves the problem by knocking the mean old troll into the river. He makes it safely across the bridge, and all of the goats get what they want—fresh green grass to eat!

 ## Focus the Conversation

Ask students to go knee-to-knee, eye-to-eye, and discuss what you included when you summarized the end of the story. Celebrate students who used body language appropriate for talking to a partner.

 ## Restate the Teaching Point

Review summarizing and the elements that make up the ending of a story:

Today, you learned how to identify what's important to remember at the end of a story—how the characters solve the problem and get what they want. Don't forget; remembering this element helps you understand what the story is about.

 ## Move to Independent Practice

Display and read the Easy Books chart. Remind children that once they have selected their easy books they need to sit at their tables or desks and read. Once they finish reading their easy books, they are free to select two more easy books. This will continue until it is time for share circle.

INDEPENDENT READING TIME

Continue to work with small groups and individuals to support their approximations with book choice.

SHARE CIRCLE

Briefly review the rules on the Speaking and Listening chart. Then start share circle by celebrating students who stayed engaged during independent reading time and found easy books to read. Ask volunteers to read a few pages of an easy book. Have the other children listen to see if each book met the criteria listed on the Easy Books chart.

▲▲▲

Calendar for Lesson Plans
WEEK 2

LESSON 6

Part 1, Book Choice: Introduce interesting books and their purpose.

Part 2, Fix-Up Strategies: Introduce or review the following strategies: point and slide to sound it out and use chunks you know.

LESSON 7

Part 1, Book Choice: Introduce interesting books and their purpose.

Part 2, Fix-Up Strategies: Review point and slide to sound it out and use chunks you know.

LESSON 8-10

Summary: Readers summarize the most important parts of a story to help them understand and remember what they have read.

Note: These lessons are repeated to provide practice in summarizing. A different book is used in each lesson.

Building Independent Readers © 2012 by Linda Lee & Mary Haymond • Scholastic Teaching Resources

Lesson 6, Part 1

Book Choice

Teaching Point: Readers read interesting books for a variety of purposes and in a variety of genres.

Weekly Conversation Skill Focus: Listening, agreeing, and naming it—naming what you agree with.

Materials:
- Easy Books chart
- Interesting Books chart
- chart paper and markers
- two high-interest nonfiction texts

Preparation:
- Create the Interesting Books chart shown below.
- Allot 20–25 minutes for students to read independently.

Interesting Books

I can read books that are interesting to me. I find them interesting because—

✰ I like the topic.

✰ I get meaning from the pictures, words, or having heard the story before.

✰ I want to read these books for a long time.

 ## Activate Prior Knowledge

Display the Easy Books and Interesting Books charts and review what students have learned about choosing these books.

Last week, you learned why and how to choose easy books. Today, you are going to learn about choosing interesting books. A book is interesting if you like the topic and can get meaning from the pictures, or words, or from having heard it before. You know a book is interesting because you want to stay with it for a very long time. Readers read interesting books because they are fun!

 ## Model the Lesson

Show the nonfiction texts that are of high interest to your students and share your purpose for reading them.

I have two interesting books that I am going to share with you. The first one is about snakes. When I was mowing my yard yesterday, I saw a snake. I don't know what kind it was. Maybe this book will help me find out.

I am going to scan the table of contents to see if that helps me. There is a section on different kinds of snakes. I am going to turn to that section. Look, this is the snake I saw. The label under the picture says "garter snake." My other interesting book has the most beautiful pictures of butterflies. I just love looking at all the details in the illustrations. During independent reading practice, I will read these books after I finish reading my easy books.

Focus the Conversation

Invite partners to turn and talk about what they know about choosing interesting books. As you listen, select one or two pairs to serve as examples. Respond by agreeing with what these students share and naming it:

✫ *I agree with you, Hailey, because you have to like the topic for a book to be interesting.*

✫ *I agree with you, Joseph, because if a book is interesting you want to read it for a long time.*

Explain to students that you just showed them the conversation skill that they will practicing this week: listening, agreeing, and naming what was shared. Emphasize how important it is for partners to listen to each other so they can name what is said.

Restate the Teaching Point

Review the purpose and reasons for choosing interesting books. Remind students to refer to the Interesting Books chart to help them select interesting books.

Move to Independent Practice

In order to slowly increase independent reading time, ask students to go book shopping for two easy books and two interesting books. After students make their selections, ask them to check in with you, so you can see who might need more assistance with book choice. Then they can sit at their tables and read.

INDEPENDENT READING TIME

At this point, students are expected to stay with their four books (two easy, two interesting) the entire time, and they will read for a total time of 20–25 minutes. Tell students to be prepared to bring their four books to share circle. Continue to work with small groups and individuals in supporting their approximations with book choice. This is when you start to get to know more about the specific interests of all your students. Ask them if there is a topic they would like to learn about and then show them how to find nonfiction books on that topic in the classroom library. Sometimes just looking through a basket of books will spark a reader's interest. As you circulate around the room, look for students who applied your teaching about interesting book choices that others could learn from:

Hailey, would you tell me about your purpose for reading today? Oh, so your cat just had kittens, and when you saw this book about cats, you knew it was the one for you. Would you mind sharing how that experience set your purpose for book choice today?

Building Independent Readers © 2012 by Linda Lee & Mary Haymond • Scholastic Teaching Resources

SHARE CIRCLE

Discuss students who you observed applying what was taught and who were engaged the entire time during independent reading.

I was watching Hailey, and she was so interested in her book. When I asked her about her book choice, she excitedly shared that her cat just had kittens. The book she chose was giving her new information about how to care for kittens. She lingered over the illustrations for a very long time.

Finally, ask students to turn-and-talk about what they learned today in terms of selecting and reading interesting books. Briefly summarize the day's learning.

Lesson 6, Part 2

Fix-Up Strategies

Teaching Point: Readers use the following fix-up strategies to predict unknown words:

- Point and slide to sound it out.
- Use chunks you know.

Weekly Conversation Skill Focus: Listening, agreeing, and naming it

Materials:
- a big book or a copy of a continuous text displayed so everyone can see it
- Fix-Up Strategies chart

Preparation:
- Add the two new strategies to the Fix-Up Strategies chart as shown below.
- Select five words in the big book or text to use in modeling the new fix-up strategies. These words must be decodable using the new fix-up strategies being taught.

Fix-Up Strategies

You use fix-up strategies to predict and confirm tricky words.
- ✫ Stop and think what would make sense.
- ✫ Look at the picture and think what would make sense.
- ✫ Reread and get your mouth ready to say the word.
- ✫ Point and slide to sound it out.
- ✫ Use chunks you know.

Activate Prior Knowledge

Display the Fix-Up Strategies chart and review the strategies you taught or reviewed last week. Next, introduce the two new strategies you added to the chart.

I am going to teach you two more fix-up strategies that will help you figure out tricky words. These new strategies are "point and slide to sound out the word" and "use chunks you know." Readers need more than one way to figure out a tricky word. If one strategy doesn't work, you can always try one or more of the others.

 ## Model the Lesson

This lesson is very similar to Lesson 1, Part 2. The only difference is that the words you select need to be decodable. Read a section of a book and model how you use the two new strategies to figure out tricky words. Stop after identifying about five words and explicitly share why you chose the strategy or strategies you used to figure out each word:

I'm having trouble with this word. Hmm . . . let me try to point and slide through it. "Point and slide through the word" reminds me to put my finger under the word and then move my finger as I blend the sounds of the letters together. Some people call this "sounding it out." Let me try it. The word sounds like apple. *I better try this one more time. Now I am going to read the sentence with the word* apple *in it: "I saw an apple on the tree." It makes sense, and the letters match, so it must be the right word. Oh, no, I am stuck on a tricky word again!* (Try pointing and sliding through the word a few times without success.) *I've tried point and slide to sound it out three times, but it's not helping me. So, I think I will try using chunks I know. I see the* -ight *chunk. I know that sounds like "ite," so the word must be* might. *Let me reread the sentence to see if it makes sense and sounds right: "Claire might go camping." It does! Hey, that strategy worked for me. I am glad I have more than one tool to solve a reading challenge.*

 ## Focus the Conversation

Talk about how it is helpful to park our own thinking when we listen to someone else so we can listen with intent to that person's ideas. When we listen with intent, we are thinking about what the other person is sharing, and our job is to respond to what they shared by naming it. Young children can be taught to listen. It takes time and practice, so begin building the foundation for growing a conversation slowly, giving children time to practice each component.

Invite students to go knee-to-knee, eye-to-eye, and take turns naming the fix-up strategies they observed you using and why you used them. Listen to their conversations and ask a few pairs to share their observations. When they share, model agreement with what they shared and named. Stress that, in order to do this, you had to park your own thinking and really listen to what was being shared.

 ## Restate the Teaching Point

Review the two new fix-up strategies you introduced in this lesson. Remind students that they can refer to the Fix-Up Strategies chart to help them figure out tricky words as they read. Point out that there are now five strategies they can use.

 Building Independent Readers © 2012 by Linda Lee & Mary Haymond • Scholastic Teaching Resources

Lesson 7, Part 1

Book Choice

Teaching Point: Readers read interesting books for a variety of purposes and in a variety of genres.

Weekly Conversation Skill Focus: Listening, agreeing, and naming it

Materials:
- Easy Books and Interesting Books charts
- an engaging text, such as *The Recess Queen* by Alexis O'Neill
- Speaking and Listening chart

Preparation:
- Allot 20–25 minutes for students to read independently.

 ## Activate Prior Knowledge

Use the charts to review what students have learned about choosing easy books and interesting books. Discuss why readers read different types of texts. Easy texts increase fluency and interesting texts allow readers to learn more about a topic.

Sometimes interesting books are so entertaining that you are willing to return to them again and again. I was thinking about your reaction when I read The Recess Queen *by Alexis O'Neill. When I finished reading it, many of you asked me if I would read it again! Old favorites are one type of interesting books! So, let's read* The Recess Queen *again.*

 ## Model the Lesson

Reread *The Recess Queen*. As you do, think aloud about what makes this such an interesting book. When you are finished, restate how returning to an old favorite can be so entertaining.

 ## Focus the Conversation

Invite students to go knee-to-knee and eye-to-eye with a partner to share what they know about reading interesting books. Remind them that if they listen carefully, they might hear their partner say something they agree with. When they do, they should agree and name what they agreed with. Again, this increases the likelihood of students listening to what's being shared during a conversation. Repeat that students will have to park their own thinking and focus on listening to their partner. Listen to the discussions and select one or two pairs who can serve as models for listening, agreeing, and naming it.

As I was listening to partners share, I heard Paige say something so smart. When she was finished sharing, her partner said, "I agree with you." Paige wanted to hear more from her partner. She remembered that it's important to name the part that you agree with. Paige encouraged her partner to say more by asking him to share what part he agreed with. Thank you, Paige, for bringing out the best in your conversation.

Restate the Teaching Point

Review easy books and interesting books and the differences between them. Tell students that these categories will guide their book choice today.

 ## Move to Independent Practice

In order to slowly increase independent reading time, again ask your students to shop for two easy and two interesting books. Then have them check in with you before they begin reading.

INDEPENDENT READING PRACTICE

Once students have selected their books and checked in with you, they sit at their tables and read. You will still need to monitor the room to offer assistance as needed.

Remind children to quickly assemble on the carpet with their books when they hear the signal to stop reading.

SHARE CIRCLE

Before children share, review the criteria on the Speaking and Listening chart. Then highlight students who stayed engaged during independent reading. Ask them to share how their passion influenced their interesting book choices. What enabled them to linger with the text for a long time?

Lesson 7, Part 2

Fix-Up Strategies

Teaching Point: Readers use the following fix-up strategies to predict unknown words:

- Point and slide to sound it out.
- Use chunks you know.

Weekly Conversation Skill Focus: Listening, agreeing, and naming it

Materials:
- a big book or a display copy of a continuous text so everyone can see it
- Fix-Up Strategies chart

Preparation:
- Select four words in the big book or text to use to model the fix-up strategies; some should be decodable.

 Building Independent Readers © 2012 by Linda Lee & Mary Haymond • Scholastic Teaching Resources

Activate Prior Knowledge

Use the Fix-Up Strategy chart to set the purpose for your lesson. Review the two new strategies introduced in Lesson 6: point and slide to sound it out and use chunks you know.

 ## Model the Lesson

Review the five fix-up strategies that readers might use to predict tricky words. Then display the big book or text you are going to read. Invite students to become your reading coaches and give you assistance by suggesting one or more of the fix-up strategies when you encounter a tricky word. Read a few pages of the book and stop at a tricky word. As children suggest a strategy, try it out. The strategy may or may not work, depending upon your goal. For example, students might suggest "point and slide through the word" with every word. Include words that are decodable so they can watch your attempt to use it and understand that this strategy doesn't always work. Ask students to suggest a different strategy until you find one that helps you understand the word. Repeat the process for all the words you selected.

 ## Focus the Conversation

Invite students to go knee-to-knee, eye-to-eye with their partner. Focus the conversation by asking them to share which strategies you used. As partners talk, listen for discussions that include the conversational moves of listening, agreeing, and naming what is agreed with.

Ask a few of these students to share their thinking with the whole group. Have them sit in the middle of a circle and replay their conversation. Tell the other students to observe as the partners listen to each other and respond with an agreement and name it. Then lead a class discussion on how listening for something you can agree with keeps you focused on what's being shared in a conversation. To do this, you also have to park your own thinking and tune in to what's being shared. You might want to take a photograph of the partnership in action and display it in your classroom as a reminder of how to hold a conversation.

 ## Restate the Teaching Point

Go over the five fix-up strategies that students now know and emphasize the importance of having a variety of strategies to use:

We now have five strategies to use when we come to a tricky word. They are:
✿ *Stop and think what would make sense.*
✿ *Look at the picture and think what word would make sense.*
✿ *Reread and get your mouth ready to say the word.*
✿ *Point and slide to sound it out.*
✿ *Use chunks you know.*
It is so important to have a variety of strategies because using just one doesn't always work.

If there is time, you can read *Brave Irene* by William Steig to students. Use the text to discuss the power of stamina and how having this quality enables one to accomplish something, even if it is hard to do!

Lessons 8, 9, and 10

Summary

Note: This lesson is repeated for three days, using a different book each day. Students need to watch and listen to several demonstrations of summarizing text. Eventually, they will be writing summaries. The ability to provide an oral summary is the foundation for later written work.

Teaching Point: Readers summarize the most important parts of a story to help them understand and remember what they have read.

Weekly Conversation Skill Focus: Listening, agreeing, and naming it

Materials:
- a different book for each lesson, such as *Shortcut* by Donald Crews, *The Recess Queen* by Alexis O'Neill, and *Owl Babies* by Martin Waddell
- Summary chart

Preparation:
- Allot 20–25 minutes for students to read independently.

Activate Prior Knowledge

Ask students to share with a partner what they have learned about summarizing a story. Make sure the Summary chart is visible to everyone.

Today, I am going to ask you to use all the things you have learned about summarizing a story. Before I begin, turn to your partner and review what is important to remember at the beginning, middle, and ending of a story. Remember, you can always read the Summary chart if you need help.

Model the Lesson/Focus the Conversation

Begin reading the text, and when there is enough information, stop and have children turn and talk about what happened at the beginning of the story: identify the characters, the setting, and what the character wants—the goal. Listen to their interactions and select a pair to share their discussion with the whole group. Make your selection based on the quality of the discussion you overhear. After the pairs have shared, model listening, agreeing, and naming something each group shared.

Continue reading and stop when there is enough information to identify what's happening in the middle of the story: what is keeping the character from reaching his or her goal and how the character tries to solve this problem. Have partners discuss what is happening in the middle of the story. Again, listen to their discussions and select pairs to share their conversation with the whole group. Model listening, agreeing, and naming the ideas shared.

Building Independent Readers © 2012 by Linda Lee & Mary Haymond • Scholastic Teaching Resources

Finish reading the story. Have partners share how the story ended: how the character solved the problem and reached his or her goal. Again, listen to partner interactions and select a pair to share their conversation with the class. Finally, invite a student to share a summary of the story with the whole group.

Restate the Teaching Point

Wrap up the lesson with something like this:

As I read the book, I stopped at different points along the way and asked you to check for understanding. You paid careful attention to the characters, the setting, and what the character wanted at the beginning of the story. Then I read the middle of the story and asked you to check for understanding by identifying the problem in the story. I finished the book and asked you to talk about how the problem got solved and how the story ended. This is what you will do every time you read a story. Remember that a summary is telling the most important parts, as Max did when he summarized the story for us.

Moving to Independent Practice

Remind students that you know where all the books in the classroom are located. If they are having any trouble finding two easy and/or two interesting books, they can ask you or their classmates for assistance.

INDEPENDENT READING PRACTICE

Have students read independently for 20–25 minutes. Don't start book clubs or guided reading yet. Your focus is still on helping students with book choice and building their reading stamina. Once they understand how to select books and display reading stamina, guided reading and book clubs can begin. We usually start our small-group work after approximately six weeks of instruction.

SHARE CIRCLE

Take the opportunity to review how to choose books wisely. Highlight a few students who applied your teaching about book choice. Celebrate those who stayed engaged during independent reading. After reviewing the Speaking and Listening chart, invite students to share one of their books, their purpose for reading it, and where they found the book in the classroom.

Calendar for Lesson Plans
WEEK 3

LESSON 11

Part 1, Book Choice: Introduce just-right books and their purpose.

Part 2, Fix-Up Strategies: Read on and then come back to the word and make a meaningful substitution.

LESSON 12

Part 1, Book Choice: Introduce just-right books and their purpose.

Part 2, Fix-Up Strategies: Read on and come back to the word and make a meaningful substitution.

LESSON 13

Summary: Create a story-map mural to remember the important characters when summarizing a story.

LESSON 14

Summary: Create a story-map mural to remember the setting when summarizing a story.

LESSON 15

Summary: Create a story-map mural to order the sequence of events when summarizing a story.

Lesson 11, Part 1

Book Choice

Teaching Point: Reading just-right books helps improve reading.

Weekly Conversation Skill Focus: Listening, agreeing, naming it, and adding on

Materials:
- Easy Books and Interesting Books charts
- chart paper and marker
- an example of a difficult book
- a collection of just-right books that matches the range of readers in your classroom (see page 128 for suggestions)
- sticky notes

Preparation:
- Create the Just-Right Books chart shown below.
- Allot about 25–30 minutes for book selection and independent reading time.

Just-Right Books

The purpose of reading a just-right book is to get better at reading.
A book is just right for you if—
- ✪ you can read most of the words most of the time.
- ✪ you can figure out tricky words using your fix-up strategies.
- ✪ you can summarize what you are reading.

 ## Activate Prior Knowledge

Use the charts to review selecting easy books and interesting books. Then display the Just-Right Books chart and set the stage for the day's lesson:

Today, I'm going to teach you how to select a just-right book. The purpose of reading a just-right book is to get better at reading. You know a book is just right because you can read most of the words, and you can use your fix-up strategies to figure out tricky words. You also understand what you are reading, and you can summarize the important parts of the book.

Model the Lesson

It is helpful to show students what to do when a book is not right for them. Ask students to watch and listen as you try to read such a book. Explain that you will use fix-up strategies to tackle any tricky words; if there are too many tricky words, you will know that the book is not just right for you. If the book is a just-right book, you will summarize it. Introduce the book you are going to read to students:

My sister loaned me this book about nursing and recommended that I read the first chapter to figure out why I eat so much candy. (Begin reading. Be sure to model when encountering tricky words.) *Wow, I am already stuck on a word in the first sentence. Let me try some strategies to figure it out. Nothing is helping me. I guess I will just skip the word and keep reading. Now I am stuck on another word, and I can't seem to figure it out. It is happening again. This book has too many tricky words for me. If I can't figure them out, then I can't understand what I am reading. I better give it back to my sister and keep on eating candy.*

Present another book to students and model how it is a just-right book for you. Use fix-up strategies to figure out three or four words, then summarize what you have read.

Focus the Conversation

Invite your students to go knee-to-knee, eye-to-eye, and talk about what makes a book just right. Encourage them to listen with intent by finding something their partner shares that they can agree with. As partners talk, capture a few examples of conversations that went well. Ask a few pairs to share their conversation with the whole group. As they share, model listening, agreeing, naming it, and then adding on to their comments by using the following stem: *"I agree with . . . and I can add on . . ."*

Restate the Teaching Point

Repeat the important concepts in today's lesson: why and how to choose a just-right book; using fix-up strategies to figure out unfamiliar words; and showing comprehension of the just-right text by summarizing it.

Move to Independent Practice

To deepen students' understanding of just-right books, compare the selection of this type of book with shopping for new shoes. Begin by asking students to think about their shoe. Here's an example:

Even though you are all in second grade, not everyone wears the same size shoes. And it doesn't really matter what size shoe you wear; the important thing is that your shoes fit. If they are too small, you will get a blister. If they are too big, they will fall off when you are running around at recess. The same is true when you are shopping for just-right books. If you want to get better at reading, the book you choose needs to be just right for you, not your classmates.

INDEPENDENT READING PRACTICE

Ask students to find two just-right books. Just-right book choice is so important that it is the sole focus of the independent reading practice in this lesson. Here, we do not ask students to select easy and interesting books. Tell children that you want them to be prepared to share one of their just-right books with the class at share circle and explain how they figured out a tricky word using fix-up strategies.

SHARE CIRCLE

Model listening, agreeing, naming it, and adding on for students. Don't expect them to use this new conversation strategy immediately. They will need a few more demonstrations before they will be able to use it. Next, ask them to share their just-right books and how they used fix-up strategies to figure out a tricky word. Highlight and celebrate the concept that students are reading a variety of just-right books, rather than books that are the same level.

Lesson 11, Part 2

Fix-Up Strategies

Teaching Point: Readers use the following fix-up strategies to predict unknown words:

- Read on and then come back to the word.
- Make a meaningful substitution.

Weekly Conversation Skill Focus: Listening, agreeing, naming it, and adding on

Materials:
- a big book or display copy of a continuous text so everyone can see it
- Fix-Up Strategies chart

Preparation:
- Add the two new strategies to the bottom of the Fix-Up Strategies chart, as shown below.
- Select five words in the text to decipher using the new fix-up strategies and some of the older strategies.

Fix-Up Strategies

You can use these fix-up strategies to predict and confirm tricky words.

- ✫ Stop and think what would make sense.
- ✫ Look at the picture and think what would make sense.
- ✫ Reread and get your mouth ready to say the word.
- ✫ Point and slide to sound it out.
- ✫ Use chunks you know.
- ✫ Read on and then come back to the word.
- ✫ Make a meaningful substitution.

⤷ Activate Prior Knowledge

Display and read the Fix-Up Strategies chart to review the strategies that students know. Then describe the two new strategies you have added to the chart. Remind students that the more fix-up strategies they know, the easier it will be for them to figure out tricky words.

⤷ Model the Lesson

Display the book you are going to read aloud. As you read it, model how you read on and come back to a word to figure it out, and also how you make a meaningful substitution for a word to solve it:

> *This word is so tricky. I think I will read on to gather more context clues to help me figure it out. I will read to the end of the sentence and think about what would make sense and sound right: "The _____ was surrounded by water." I bet the word is* island! *That makes sense because an island is surrounded by water.*

Next, model how to make a meaningful substitution. Select a proper noun in the text for this demonstration. Explain how substituting a name doesn't change the meaning of the text.

As you continue to read, also use some of the more familiar fix-up strategies to figure out words. Explicitly share why you chose each fix-up strategy or strategies.

⤷ Focus the Conversation

Before partners begin their discussions, model this week's conversational skill focus: listening, agreeing, naming it, and adding on. Then invite students to go knee-to-knee, eye-to-eye, and name the strategies they saw you use. Ask a few to share their observations with the class. Highlight students who went knee-to-knee, made eye contact, and stayed engaged by agreeing with something their partner shared and adding on to it.

⤷ Restate the Teaching Point

Sum up the day's lesson by reviewing the two new fix-up strategies. Emphasize that knowing more strategies will help students figure out tricky words and will improve their reading comprehension.

Lesson 12, Part 1

Book Choice

Teaching Point: Reading just-right books helps improve our reading.
Weekly Conversation Skill Focus: Listening, agreeing, naming it, and adding on
Materials:
- Easy Books, Interesting Books, and Just-Right Books charts
- a collection of just-right books (see page 128)
- sticky notes

Preparation: • Select three tricky words in the text. Write each word on a sticky note and place it on the corresponding text page.
• Allot 25–30 minutes for students to read independently.

 ## Activate Prior Knowledge

Review the definitions of easy and interesting books and go over what your students have learned about choosing these types of books. Then state your teaching point for the mini-lesson by reading the definition of a just-right book on the chart. Emphasize that a just-right text is one that is not too difficult. Also remind students that with just-right books, readers solve challenges using fix-up strategies to increase comprehension.

 ## Model the Lesson

Introduce the text you are going to read aloud. Explain that it is a just-right text for you. As you come to a page with a sticky note, model how you would use one or more of the fix-up strategies to decode the tricky word:

I was reading this just-right book after school, and I wanted to show you three places where I used fix-up strategies to figure out tricky words. I put sticky notes on the pages where I did my good work. Here's my first sticky note and the page I placed it on. I was stuck on the word choice, *and I figured it out by reading on and coming back to the word. I wanted to share the word with you and how I figured it out, so I wrote it on the sticky note and placed it on the page. The book was just right for me because when I came to a tricky word I could figure it out.*

Continue this demonstration for two other words you have marked in the book.

 ## Focus the Conversation

Invite your students to have a conversation with their partner by asking each other if there was anything they agreed with in your demonstration and if they could add to that. Listen for a conversation that includes the aspects of this week's conversation skill focus. Ask those pairs of students to replay their conversation for the entire group.

Restate the Teaching Point

Restate the teaching point of today's lesson:

Reading just-right books helps you get better at reading. You only have to figure out a few tricky words, and you can understand what you read. You are becoming an independent problem-solver when you figure out tricky words.

Move to Independent Practice

Inform students that your expectation is for them to be prepared to share a just-right book and how they figured out a tricky word in it at share circle:

Today, I am going to give each of you three sticky notes. When you figure out a tricky word in your just-right book, write it on a sticky note. Leave it on the page where you did your amazing work. Some of you will get to share about your sticky note evidence at share circle.

INDEPENDENT READING PRACTICE

Students select two easy books, two just-right books, and two interesting books. Continue supporting students in small groups or individually with their book choice and monitor the room to reinforce engagement and independence.

SHARE CIRCLE

Ask a few students to share the word on their sticky note and how they figured it out. Celebrate those who stayed engaged during independent reading.

Lesson 12, Part 2

Fix-Up Strategies

Teaching Point: Readers use the following fix-up strategies to predict unknown words:

- Read on and come back to the word.
- Make a meaningful substitution.

Weekly Conversation Skill Focus: Listening, agreeing, naming it, and adding on

Materials:
- a big book or a display copy of a continuous text, such as *Dragon Tales* by Dav Pilkey
- Fix-Up Strategies chart
- a read-aloud book, such as *Walk On!* by Marla Frazee

Preparation:
- Select five words in the text to use to model fix-up strategies.
- Add the two new strategies to the Fix-Up Strategies chart.

 ## Activate Prior Knowledge

Use the Fix-Up Strategies chart to review the two new strategies and to set the purpose for this lesson.

 Building Independent Readers © 2012 by Linda Lee & Mary Haymond • Scholastic Teaching Resources

Model the Lesson

Display the text you are going to read to students. Invite them to become reading coaches and give you assistance by suggesting one or more of the fix-up strategies on the chart when you encounter an unfamiliar word. As you read, model getting stuck on the five words you've previously selected. Before you ask for assistance, have students turn and talk to their partner about the strategies they think you should try. Then call on children to suggest a strategy and ask them why they selected the particular strategy or strategies. Try their suggestions and discuss whether each worked. Model the conversation skill of listening, agreeing, naming it, and adding on when appropriate.

 ## Focus the Conversation

Invite students to go knee-to-knee and eye-to-eye. Focus conversation by asking them to share how they decided which strategy to suggest, even if they weren't called on. As partners talk, listen for exchanges that include the weekly conversation skill focus of listening, agreeing, naming it, and adding on. Ask two pairs to share their conversation with the whole group. Lead a class discussion on how listening for something you can agree with, naming what it is, and adding on proves that you are really listening to your partner and thinking about what he or she is sharing.

 ## Restate the Teaching Point

Review how reading on and then coming back to a word and making a meaningful substitution have helped students figure out unfamiliar words.

If there is time, read *Walk On!* by Marla Frazee. Use the text to discuss the power of stamina and how having this quality enables one to learn something new, even if it is hard to do!

Lesson 13

Summary

Teaching Points: Readers do the following to help them summarize:

- They remember the important characters.
- They use what they know about the structure of text as a strategy for summarizing.

Weekly Conversation Skill Focus: Listening, agreeing, naming it, and adding on

Materials:
- Summary chart
- *Owl Babies* by Martin Waddell, or a text with a setting that doesn't change and characters that are easy to draw
- paper and paint or crayons
- cotton swabs
- sticky notes

Preparation:
- Make a model of an owl (or of the main character in the text you choose).
- Allot 25–30 minutes for students to read independently.

 ## Activate Prior Knowledge

Read the Summary chart. Ask students to turn and talk about what they have learned about how to summarize text. Also have them tell why this is important.

 ## Model the Lesson

Explain that making story-map murals can help readers remember important ideas in a book. Display *Owl Babies* or another text you chose. Tell students that you will read aloud the story and everyone will work together to summarize it:

To help you remember the important parts of the story to include in your summary, we are going to make a story-map mural to hang in our classroom. We will label the mural so you will always remember what to include when you summarize a story. We can't finish the story-map mural project in one day, so we will summarize the beginning of Owl Babies *today. As I read the story, think about the characters. When I am finished reading the story, I want each one of you to create an owl to go on the story-map mural.*

After reading the beginning of the text, ask students to identify the main characters. Provide materials and have them create their own renderings of the characters. For example, they can use cotton swabs as paintbrushes to create feathers on an owl.

 ## Restate the Teaching Point

Make the connection between making a story-map mural and remembering the important parts of a story in order to summarize it.

 ## Move to Independence Practice

Tell students that they should select and read two just-right books and be prepared to share evidence that they solved a tricky word using fix-up strategies. Give students access to sticky notes for this work.

INDEPENDENT READING PRACTICE

Students select and read their just-right books, marking the places where they used fix-up strategies to help them read a tricky or an unfamiliar word.

SHARE CIRCLE

Celebrate students who stayed engaged during independent reading time. Invite them to share how they figured out a tricky word in their just-right book.

Lesson 14

Summary

Teaching Point: Readers use the setting to help them summarize a story.
Weekly Conversation Skill Focus: Listening, agreeing, naming it, and adding on
Materials:
- Summary chart
- text from Lesson 13
- black butcher paper (24 inches x 36 inches)
- small piece of black paper (12 inches x 18 inches)
- green construction paper
- brown construction paper
- scissors

Preparation:
- Cut the black paper into five equal-sized panels.
- Cut a tree with branches out of brown paper and leaves out of green paper.
- Allot 25–30 minutes for students to read independently.

↪ Activate Prior Knowledge

Use the Summary chart to review how to summarize a story. Ask students to use the artwork they created in Lesson 13 to tell about the character in the text.

Remind students how identifying the setting also helps them summarize the beginning of a text and remember what they have read:

To help you remember the important parts to include in our summary of Owl Babies, *we are going to continue to work on our story-map mural. Yesterday, you created the character for our* Owl Babies *story-map mural. Today, you will create the setting. As I reread the story, think about the setting. Where does this story take place? When I am finished reading the story, each of you will work in a small group to create the setting.*

Model the Lesson

Read *Owl Babies* from the beginning. When you are finished, facilitate a dialogue with students about the setting. What is important to include in the story-map mural and what can be left out?

For the entire story-map mural, you will need five setting panels:

✯ Panel 1: Shows the setting at the beginning of the story.
✯ Panels 2–4: Show the setting in the middle of the story.
✯ Panel 5: Shows the setting at the end of the story.

Our example, *Owl Babies*, has a consistent setting, which is why we selected it for this project. It is set in the forest at night. To represent this, we cut a large sheet of black paper into five equal-size panels. Each of the five panels will show a brown tree with green leaves. To help students succeed, create a small version of the setting as a scaffold. Explain that the black paper represents the night. Then glue a brown tree with broad limbs on the black paper. Glue green leaves on the tree branches. Then explain:

You get to work with a group to create a panel just like the one you saw me make. The only difference will be the size of your panel. It will be a lot bigger than this one I just made.

Divide the class into five groups. Each group will create a panel for the setting. When they are finished, tell students where to place their panels. ***Note:*** After school you will select three owls to be glued on each panel. The panels should be ready by the next day's mini-lesson.

 ## Restate the Teaching Point

Wrap up this part of the lesson by talking about how the setting helps readers summarize and remember what they are reading.

 ## Move to Independent Practice

Before the groups begin work on their panels, tell students that when they finish they should select and read their just-right books.

INDEPENDENT READING PRACTICE

When students finish their group work, tell them to select two just-right books. They should read until all the groups have finished their work on the mural panels, and use sticky notes to mark places where they encountered and solved tricky words.

SHARE CIRCLE

Invite students to share their sticky note evidence to show that they can use fix-up strategies to figure out tricky words.

Lesson 15

Summary

Teaching Point: Readers use sequence of events when they are summarizing a story.

Weekly Conversation Skill Focus: Listening, agreeing, naming it, and adding on

Materials:
- Summary chart
- story-map mural panels created in Lesson 14
- glue
- marker
- sticky notes
- index cards

Preparation:
- Allot 25–30 minutes for students to read independently.

 ## Activate Prior Knowledge

Display the Summary chart. Review how the setting helps readers summarize the story and remember what they are reading. Next, explain how identifying the important parts of a story—beginning, middle, and end— helps readers understand and remember what they have read. Knowing the order of events is an important part of summarizing text:

Here are the panels you created yesterday. I have attached three owls to each panel. Today, I need you to help me write a summary. Listen carefully as I reread Owl Babies. *Your job is to capture the most important parts that happened at the beginning, middle, and end of this story. Then we will put that information on our panels to create a story-map mural.*

Model the Lesson/Focus the Conversation

Display each panel or set of panels and ask students to turn and talk about what they think should go on it. Listen to the conversations and select someone to share a brief summary for each part of the story. Discuss what to include on the panel or set of panels, for example:

What should I write about the first panel? It shows what happened at the beginning of the story: the characters, the setting, and what the characters wanted. Turn and talk to your partner about what happened at the beginning of the story.

The next three panels are for the most important events that happened in the middle of the story. They show the problem. Turn and talk to you partner about what to include on each panel. The last panel shows what happened at the end of the story. Turn and talk to your partner about what I should write about how the story ended.

Record students' responses on sticky notes. Later, type their responses on index cards and attach them to the panels. Write students' responses about each part of the story on the appropriate panels.

 ## Restate the Teaching Point

Hang the story-map mural. Use the information in it to summarize the text. Remind students that they can use the story-map mural to help remind them of how to summarize so they can understand and remember what they read.

Each day during independent reading practice, invite a few students to use the mural to practice providing a brief summary of a story. If you don't provide time for students to use the mural, you have accomplished little more than creating a lovely display.

 ## Move to Independent Practice

Remind students to use what they have learned about book choice to select just-right books. Have sticky notes available so they can mark places in the text where they solved tricky words.

INDEPENDENT READING PRACTICE

Students read their just-right books for 25–30 minutes. Circulate around the room to provide encouragement and assistance as needed. You may still need to provide small-group support to help students find just-right books or to record how they solved tricky words using the fix-up strategies on their sticky notes.

SHARE CIRCLE

The focus of sharing is just-right books and how students figured out a tricky word.

Calendar for Lesson Plans
WEEK 4

Note: In Week 4, the order of the lessons is switched; the fix-up strategies appear first. Students have learned all the strategies and will use that knowledge to predict and confirm unfamiliar words as they read their just-right books.

LESSON 16

Part 1, Fix-Up Strategies: Introduce cross-checking using the How Many Ways of Knowing game. (See page 31.)

Part 2, Book Choice:
Just-Right Books: Introduce What's Helpful/What's Not Helpful chart.

LESSON 17

Part 1, Fix-Up Strategies: Introduce cross-checking using How Many Ways of Knowing game.

Part 2, Book Choice:
Just-Right Books: Continue What's Helpful/What's Not Helpful chart.

LESSON 18

Summary: Introduce how to use a story map to remember the important parts at the beginning of a story.

LESSON 19

Summary: Introduce how to use a story map to remember the important parts in the middle of a story.

LESSON 20

Summary: Introduce how to use a story map to remember the important parts at the end of a story.

Lesson 16, Part 1

Fix-Up Strategies

Teaching Point: Readers use fix-up strategies to cross-check by predicting and confirming unfamiliar words.

Weekly Conversation Skill Focus: I don't understand . . .

Materials:
- Fix-Up Strategies chart
- display copy of continuous text
- sticky notes

Preparation:
- Cover up five words in the text you are using for the lesson. Leave the first letter, blends, or digraphs uncovered so you can use "get your mouth ready" as a fix-up strategy.
- Add the last two reading strategies to the Fix-Up Strategies chart as shown below.

Fix-Up Strategies

You can use strategies to predict and confirm tricky words.

- ✰ Stop and think what would make sense.
- ✰ Look at the pictures and think what would make sense.
- ✰ Reread and get your mouth ready to say the word.
- ✰ Point and slide to sound it out.
- ✰ Use chunks you know.
- ✰ Read on and then come back to the word.
- ✰ Make a meaningful substitution.
- ✰ Ask someone.
- ✰ Always ask:

  Does it make sense?

  Does it sound right?

  Does it look right?

  How do you know?

Building Independent Readers © 2012 by Linda Lee & Mary Haymond • Scholastic Teaching Resources

Activate Prior Knowledge

Review the list of fix-up strategies you have previously taught. Remind students how they can use these strategies to predict unfamiliar words when they read. Then read the new strategies printed on the chart:

I have added two new strategies to our chart. The first new strategy is to ask someone. But we only ask someone to tell us a word if we have tried all the other strategies and none of them worked. If someone wants you to tell him or her a word, be sure to ask what strategies he or she has already tried. You only get better at reading by trying to solve your own reading challenges first. The last strategy listed on the chart will be the focus of our lessons from now on. We have learned how to predict tricky words. Now we are going to learn how to know whether the word makes sense, sounds right, and looks right. When we do this, we confirm our prediction. We see whether our prediction was right. We ask ourselves questions to confirm our predictions: Does it make sense? Does it sound right? Does it look right? How do I know?

 ## Model the Lesson

In preparation for Lesson 17, in which students play the How Many Ways of Knowing game, model predicting and confirming unfamiliar words in a text. Read aloud the text, stopping at the five words you have pre-selected and modeling how to use fix-up strategies to predict and confirm the words. Explicitly share why you chose the strategies you used to figure out and confirm each unfamiliar word. The reason the words are covered (except for the beginning sound) is to show students how to use structure and meaning to decipher the words. As you uncover each word, use its visual features to help predict and confirm:

I am stuck on this word. I think I will look at the picture and think what word would make sense here. Now, I am going to reread and get my mouth ready. The word begins with the letter g. I predict that the word is garden. To help me be sure the word makes sense and sounds right, I am going to insert the word, reread the sentence, and then read on: "The mother watered the flowers in her garden." It does sound right and make sense. Now I will uncover the word and see if there is a match. Yes, the word I predicted looks just like the word in the book! Watch me write down what I did on a sticky note so I will remember what strategies worked to predict and confirm the word. I will use initials for the strategies I used. That way, it won't take too much time away from my reading. I'll use the these codes: p.c. for "picture clues," r.s. for "reread the sentence," g.m.r. for "get your mouth ready," and r.c.b. for "read on and come back." Remember: It doesn't matter how you code the strategies as long as you know and remember what your code means.

 ## Focus the Conversation

Invite students to have a conversation by asking each other if there was anything they didn't understand from your demonstration:

I gave you a lot of information to think about. Maybe I did or said things you don't understand. When you turn and talk today, ask your partner if there was anything he or she didn't understand. You may or may not be able to clarify it. When your discussion is finished, we will see who can help you out.

Listen to the pairs to capture a conversation that includes a discussion of something in your teaching that needs to be clarified. Invite the partners to replay their conversation for their peers and clarify any misconceptions:

I was listening to Marissa and Clayton share. Clayton said he didn't understand what I meant by creating codes for the strategies. Marissa explained that it was kind of like the plus and minus signs in math. Instead of writing the word plus *or* minus, *mathematicians use symbols because it is quicker. You can use the first letter of each word in the strategy to make your code. It is quicker than writing all the words. The most important thing is that you know what your code means.*

 Restate the Teaching Point

Remind students that the fix-up strategies can help them predict unfamiliar words in a text and confirm their predictions.

Lesson 16, Part 2

Book Choice

Teaching Point: Readers read just-right books to get better at reading.

Weekly Conversation Skill Focus: I don't understand . . .

Materials:
- Easy Books, Interesting Books, and Just-Right Books charts
- What's Helpful/What's Not Helpful chart, as shown below
- chart paper and marker
- just-right text to read aloud to students
- sticky notes

Preparation:
- Draw a T-chart on chart paper. Label the left column "What's Helpful" and the right column "What's Not Helpful," as shown below. See page 41 for a discussion of this chart.
- Select several words in the just-right text to use for modeling fix-up strategies.
- Allot 30–35 minutes for students to read independently.

What's Helpful	What's Not Helpful

Building Independent Readers © 2012 by Linda Lee & Mary Haymond • Scholastic Teaching Resources

Activate Prior Knowledge

Read the definitions of easy books, interesting books, and just-right books on the charts and review what your students have learned about choosing books. For this lesson, focus on the definition of a just-right book. Emphasize that a just-right text is not too difficult. Remind students that with these books, if readers experience a reading challenge, they can solve it using fix-up strategies to maintain comprehension. Remember that a just-right book is considered to be at the reader's instructional level or a bit easier. Explain that you are going to show students how you use reading strategies to solve reading challenges in a just-right book.

 ## Model the Lesson

Read aloud the just-right text. As you encounter the tricky words you have pre-selected, use fix-up strategies to figure them out and then confirm your predictions. Mark the pages that contain these words with sticky notes; write each word and code the fix-up strategy or strategies you used. For example, you could use *p.c.* for "picture clues," *r.s.* for "reread the sentence," *g.m.r.* for "get your mouth ready," and *r.c.b.* for "read on and come back." Tell students that it doesn't matter how they code the strategies as long as they know what their code means.

 ## Focus the Conversation

Ask students if they observed something you did when you were reading a just-right text that they didn't understand. Explain that when we don't understand something, we may ask the speaker a question using this stem: "I don't understand . . ."

 ## Restate the Teaching Point

Repeat the importance of just-right books:

Take care when you select your just-right books today. They are the most important books in your book bag because every time you read them, you get better at reading.

 ## Move to Independent Practice

Before students choose an easy book, an interesting book, and a just-right book to read independently, discuss the importance of building reading stamina and avoiding distractions:

We all know that practice will make us better readers. Some things help us build stamina, and some things take away our stamina. For example, when I am reading a book at home and the television is too loud, I can't stay focused. Today, when you have settled in with your books, take time to notice what is helping you stay focused and what's causing distractions. We will discuss these during share circle.

INDEPENDENT READING PRACTICE

Have students find an easy book, an interesting book, and a just-right book. They will then read them independently for approximately 30–35 minutes. Inform students that your expectation is for them to be prepared to tell about a just-right book at share circle.

SHARE CIRCLE

Select students to share their just-right book choice with the rest of the class. Repeat the point that students' just-right books are not all at the same level. Then discuss their focus during independent reading practice by asking students what was helpful and what was not helpful during that time. List their comments on sticky notes and post on the What's Helpful/What's Not Helpful chart. At this point, the chart will be a rough draft. It is important to let students create the criteria for this chart and recognize that it will be built over time. Now that they have had experience with independent reading time for a few weeks, they have developed a sense of what is helping them build stamina and what is taking away their stamina. They will be more than happy to describe positive behaviors. End each share circle this week by adding to this chart.

Lesson 17, Part 1

Fix-Up Strategies

Teaching Point: Readers use fix-up strategies to cross-check by predicting and confirming unfamiliar words.

Weekly Conversation Skill Focus: I don't understand . . .

Materials:
- Fix-Up Strategies chart
- display copy of continuous text
- sticky notes

Preparation:
- Cover five words in the text. Leave the initial sound, blend, or digraph uncovered.
- Review how to teach the How Many Ways of Knowing game. (See page 31.)

 ## Activate Prior Knowledge

Review the strategies on the Fix-Up Strategies chart. Remind students how they can use the strategies to predict and confirm unfamiliar words. Explain that, from now on, you will be focusing on the last strategy on the chart:

We have learned how to predict tricky words. Now we are going to learn how to know if the word makes sense, sounds right, and looks right. Remember that we call this "confirming our prediction."

 Building Independent Readers © 2012 by Linda Lee & Mary Haymond • Scholastic Teaching Resources

Model the Lesson

Explain that, to use the last strategy on the Fix-Up Strategies chart, you are going to teach students a game called How Many Ways of Knowing. As you read the text and come to an unfamiliar word, stop and ask students to help you figure it out:

Teacher: *I am stuck on this word. Sarah, what is your prediction for the word?*

Sarah: *I predict that the word is* cookies.

Teacher: (writes the word on a sticky note) *I'll write down your prediction. Which fix-up strategy or strategies did you use to predict the word?*

Sarah: *I looked at the picture clues and thought about what makes sense. The picture shows the mother pulling a pan of cookies from the oven. I also read on and then came back to the word.*

Teacher: (writes strategies on the sticky note, using code) *I'll use a code to write down the strategies. How did you confirm your prediction?*

Sarah: *I confirmed it by reading on. The word made sense and sounded right.*

Teacher: (uncovers word) *Now I will uncover the word and look carefully to see if it matches Sarah's word. Yes, the word she predicted looks just like the word in the book!*

Continue the game by reading and asking for students' assistance with the covered words.

 Focus the Conversation

Invite students to have a conversation by asking each other if there was anything they didn't understand from the game:

When you turn and talk today, ask your partner if there was anything he or she didn't understand. You may or may not be able to clarify it. When your discussion is finished, we will see who can help out.

Listen to the pairs to capture a conversation that includes a discussion of something in the game that needs to be clarified. Invite partners to replay their conversation for their peers. Clarify any misconceptions.

 Restate the Teaching Point

Review the steps in the How Many Ways of Knowing game and how it helps readers use the fix-up strategies to predict and confirm unfamiliar words.

Note: We recommend that you continue playing How Many Ways of Knowing until you have evidence that your students are cross-checking with at least two strategies. You can gather this information from running record data as well as your observations during reading conferences and guided-reading groups. Children in guided-reading groups experience more success because, when they come to an unfamiliar word, they receive a prompt and know what to do. A common language has been developed in the group. They have observed a skilled reader use the strategies and understand what the prompt requires of them.

Later, it won't be necessary to cover the words you are using for the lesson. Again, we teach students to use the visual first. All readers do this instinctively because we don't read with our eyes shut. However, students need to have alternatives when point and slide through the word doesn't work.

Lesson 17, Part 2

Book Choice

Teaching Point: Readers read just-right books to improve their reading.

Weekly Conversation Skill Focus: I don't understand . . .

Materials:
- Easy Books, Interesting Books, and Just-Right Books charts
- What's Helpful/What's Not Helpful chart
- a display copy of a just-right text
- sticky notes
- a sheet of chart paper on an easel
- *Wolf!* by Rebecca Bloom

Preparation:
- Cover five words in the text you are using for the lesson. Leave the initial sound, blend, or digraph uncovered.
- Allot 30–35 minutes for students to read independently.

Activate Prior Knowledge

Read the definitions of easy books, interesting books, and just-right books and review what students have learned about choosing books. As in Lesson 16, focus on the definition of a just-right book: Just-right text is not too difficult; if readers do experience a reading challenge, they can solve it using fix-up strategies so comprehension is always maintained.

Model the Lesson

Explain that you are going to show students how you use fix-up strategies to solve reading challenges in a just-right book. Model reading the just-right text. When you come to a covered word, use fix-up strategies to predict the word and confirm your prediction. Write your prediction and codes for the strategies you used on a sticky note and place it on the page. Tell students that they will be doing this later during their independent reading practice when they read their just-right books.

Focus the Conversation

Ask students if they observed something you did when you were reading the just-right text that they didn't understand. Remind them that when we don't understand something, we can ask the speaker a question using this stem: "I don't understand . . ."

Building Independent Readers © 2012 by Linda Lee & Mary Haymond • Scholastic Teaching Resources

Restate the Teaching Point

Remind students why and how to select just-right books.

 Move to Independent Practice

Give two sticky notes to each student so they can write their predictions and confirmations for two unfamiliar words they encounter in their just-right books:

Today, I have sticky notes for you to use. I will give each of you two so you can write down how you figured out two tricky words. You get to create your own code for the strategies you used to predict and confirm these words. You can use any code, as long as you can read and remember it. Look at the Fix-Up Strategies chart if you need to. When you come to share circle, we'll put all our sticky notes on this piece of chart paper. Won't it be fun to see all of our good work!

Independent work time is most successful if you review the What's Helpful/What's Not Helpful chart before you send your students off to work independently. Ask them to be prepared to discuss what was helpful and what was not during independent reading time and to add those thoughts to the What's Helpful/What's Not Helpful chart.

INDEPENDENT READING PRACTICE

Students choose easy, just-right, and interesting books and then read them for approximately 30–35 minutes. Remind students to stack their books in the order they are to read them: easy books first, followed by just-right books, and interesting books last. As students read, circulate around the room helping with book choice and the use of sticky notes.

SHARE CIRCLE

Give students a few minutes to post their sticky notes on the sheet of chart paper. Celebrate this evidence of students' use of fix-up strategies:

Isn't this chart amazing! Look at the reading power in this classroom. You collected evidence to prove you know how to predict and confirm tricky words.

Ask two students to share their sticky notes with the rest of the class. Invite them to add more suggestions to the What's Helpful/What's Not Helpful chart and to make any changes.

If time allows, read *Wolf!* by Rebecca Bloom. This text can be used to model the power of stamina. Link the text to the importance of practice. If we want to get better at anything we do, we have to practice. That holds true for reading.

Lesson 18

Summary

Teaching Point: Readers can use a story map to remember the important parts at the beginning of a story.

Weekly Conversation Skill Focus: I don't understand . . .

Materials:
- a text, such as *The Little Red Hen* by Lucinda McQueen, or any on page 36
- Summary chart
- 8½-in. x 14-in. legal-size paper
- sticky notes

Preparation:
- Read about making a story map on page 34.
- Fold the paper into thirds to create a story map.
- Allot 30–35 minutes for students to read independently.

 ## Activate Prior Knowledge

Read the Summary chart to review how identifying the elements of story grammar helps determine what is important to remember in the story.

 ## Model the Lesson

Display the text you are going to read aloud and explain that you are going to make a story map to help remember the important parts of this story: what happens at the beginning, the middle, and the end. Show students the story map:

> *Today, we are going to make a story map to help us remember the important parts of* The Little Read Hen. *A story map helps us remember the important parts. On the back of our story map, I will write the title of the story and the author's name.*

Read the beginning of the story and show students how to complete the story map to show the beginning: Write the label "Beginning" in the first third of the story map. Identify and sketch the character(s), setting, and goal in the map. Then write a brief description of this information underneath:

> *Watch me sketch the Little Red Hen in her kitchen. She wants to make bread. Next, I will write a short description of where she is and what she wants. This will help me remember the important parts of the beginning of the story.*

 ## Focus the Conversation

After modeling the lesson, invite students to talk to their partner and share anything they didn't understand. Listen to the conversations and capture any discussions that include "I don't understand . . ."

Building Independent Readers © 2012 by Linda Lee & Mary Haymond • Scholastic Teaching Resources

statements. Ask those pairs to share their conversation with the whole group. Clarify any information that students don't understand.

Restate the Teaching Point

Explain the purpose of creating a story map:

A story map helps readers remember what's important in a story. We made a story map when we created the mural for Owl Babies. *This story map it is smaller and only has three panels.*

Move to Independent Practice

Review the What's Helpful/What's Not Helpful chart. Then ask students to draw and write their own interpretation of the beginning of the story you read to them. (Emergent writers may accomplish the task by labeling their drawings or copying what you wrote.) For the rest of their independent reading practice, they will select and read their books. Pass out sticky notes so they can capture evidence of their fix-up strategy use.

INDEPENDENT READING PRACTICE

After working on the beginning of their story map, students find two easy, two just-right, and two interesting books to read independently for approximately 30–35 minutes. Remind them to use sticky notes to record the fix-up strategies they used to figure out tricky words. As you observe their work, select students who have completed exemplary work to share it.

SHARE CIRCLE

Invite the students you selected to share the first section of their story maps. Add any new information to the What's Helpful/What's Not Helpful chart or make other changes that students suggest. Ask a few students to tell what fix-up strategies they used while they were reading.

Lesson 19

Summary

Teaching Point: Readers use story maps to remember the important parts in the middle of a story.
Weekly Conversation Skill Focus: I don't understand . . .
Materials:
- Summary chart
- text from Lesson 18
- story map from Lesson 18

	• What's Helpful/What's Not Helpful chart
	• sticky notes
Preparation:	• Allot 30–35 minutes for students to read independently.

Activate Prior Knowledge

Use the Summary chart to review how identifying the elements of story grammar helps readers determine what is important to remember in a story. Focus students' attention on the elements that are important in the middle of a story.

Model the Lesson

Continue reading the story you began in Lesson 18. When you finish, sketch what's important in the middle of the story in the second panel of the story map. Label this section, "Middle." Your sketch should include the setting, character(s), and one event that exemplifies the problem that the character(s) faces:

The Little Red Hen wants help baking bread, but no one will help her. That is the problem that she faces and that keeps her from reaching her goal. I won't show each scene because that wouldn't be a summary. That would be a retell. So, I am going to draw the event where the Little Red Hen asks the other characters if they will help her bake the bread. I'll show the lazy characters with speech bubbles saying, "Not I."

Then add a short written description of what happened or label the most important parts (setting, characters, and problem).

Focus the Conversation

After your demonstration, invite students to draw and write about their interpretation of the middle of the book. Ask them to talk to their partner and discuss what they don't understand about this part of the story or the story map. Provide an opportunity for partners to share their questions so you can clarify meaning.

Restate the Teaching Point

Restate the purpose of a story map and how it helps readers remember the important elements in the middle of a story.

Move to Independent Practice

Before sending students off to work independently, review the tasks you expect them to do: complete the middle section of their story map; select two easy, two just-right, and two interesting books; and use sticky notes to show the fix-up strategies they used as they read their books. A quick review of the What's Helpful/What's Not Helpful chart is a proactive strategy to promote success during independent work time.

INDEPENDENT READING PRACTICE

As you observe students, select several to share the middle portion of their story maps during share circle. Help with book selection and fix-up strategies as necessary.

SHARE CIRCLE

Invite students to share the middle section of their story map. Add any comments or make any changes to the What's Helpful/What's Not Helpful chart. Quickly comment on the fix-up strategies you noticed students writing on sticky notes.

Lesson 20

Summary

Teaching Point: Readers use story maps to remember the important parts at the end of a story.

Weekly Conversation Skill Focus: I don't understand . . .

Materials:
- text from Lesson 19
- Summary chart
- story map from Lesson 19
- What's Helpful/What's Not Helpful chart
- sticky notes

Preparation:
- Allot 30–35 minutes for students to read independently.

 ## Activate Prior Knowledge

Use the Summary chart to review how identifying the elements of story grammar helps readers determine what is important to remember in the story. Focus students' attention on the important element at the end of a story—its solution.

 ## Model the Lesson

Tell students that to help summarize the story, you are going to reread the beginning and middle of *The Little Red Hen* before finishing the story and completing your story map. Rereading the story now may seem redundant, but it provides essential modeling. Explain to students that it's important to reread their books because every time readers return to a book, they take away something new.

After reading the book, complete the story map. Write the label, "Ending," in the final third. Draw a sketch that shows the end of the story and how the problem was resolved. Then write a brief description of the end of the story that includes how the problem the character encountered was solved so the goal was reached. After you complete the story map, use it to give a complete summary of *The Little Red Hen*.

 ## Focus the Conversation

After your demonstration, invite students to draw and write their interpretations of the end of the story. Have partners talk about anything they don't understand about creating the story map for the ending. Ask a few volunteers to share their questions so you can clarify meaning.

 ## Restate the Teaching Point

Restate the purpose of a story map and how it helps readers remember the important elements in the end of a story. Putting the beginning, middle, and ending together helps readers summarize the entire story.

 ## Move to Independent Practice

Before sending students off to work independently, review the tasks you expect them to do: complete the end of their story map; select two easy, two just-right, and two interesting books; and use sticky notes to show the fix-up strategies they used as they read their books. A quick review of the What's Helpful/What's Not Helpful chart is a proactive strategy to promote success during independent work time.

INDEPENDENT READING PRACTICE

As you observe students, select two who will use their story maps to summarize the story during share circle. Help with book selection and fix-up strategies as necessary.

SHARE CIRCLE

Have the two students you selected share their story maps and summaries. Then invite partners to take turns giving a summary using their story maps. At the end of share circle, ask the class if there is anything that needs to be added to the What's Helpful/What's Not Helpful chart. After today, you are going to publish the chart and display it in the classroom. Students will follow the criteria that they generated for the chart during independent work time. It is helpful to hang the chart close to where you teach your mini- lessons. Again, independent work time is most successful if you remember to read the chart before you send your students off to work independently. A sample chart is shown on page 41.

Calendar for Lesson Plans
WEEK 5

LESSON 21

Book Choice: Introduce book bags and the variety of genres and reading purposes.

LESSON 22

Fix-Up Strategies: Use fix-up strategies to predict and confirm tricky words.

LESSON 23

Summary: Introduce the difference between an oral summary and a retell.

LESSON 24

Summary: Explain the difference between audiences for an oral summary and a retell.

LESSON 25

Summary: Review the difference between an oral summary and a retell.

Lesson 21

Book Choice

Teaching Point: Readers read texts at different levels for a variety of purposes and in a variety of genres.

Weekly Conversational Skill Focus: Disagreeing

Materials:
- Easy Books, Just-Right Books, and Interesting Books charts
- book bags or book boxes (two-gallon zip-lock plastic bags, cloth bags, or plastic bags, cardboard boxes)
- indelible markers, labels
- sticky notes

Preparation:
- Write a student's name on each book bag or book box or on a label to place on the bag or box.
- Allot 35–45 minutes for students to read independently.

INTRODUCING BOOK BAGS OR BOOK BOXES

When students are confident about the types of books to read and can make appropriate book selections most of the time, give each of them a book bag or a book box to keep their books in for the week. At this point, book choice mini-lessons move from twice a week to once a week. Students select the books for the week on Monday and keep them until Friday.

The book choice mini-lesson should be the only lesson taught on Mondays. This is a change of routine, and students will need time and extra support with book choice. Because they will keep their books for the entire week, you will need to be vigilant about helping them learn to select appropriate books. On Fridays, students return the books that they no longer want to read.

The following Monday, students select new books so they have a total of five or six books to read for the week: two easy books, two just-right books, and one or two interesting books. This process is followed weekly for the remainder of the year. As the year progresses, some students will no longer need the support of interesting books to keep them engaged for the 35–45 and 45–50 minutes of independent reading time. Help other students move from six books a week to reading one or two books of their own choice. Some may not need fluency practice, so guide them away from easy books. Be on the lookout for students who spend too much time looking through interesting books and encourage them to spend more time with just-right books. In order to meet the individual needs of your students, you ultimately set the criteria for book selection for each child.

Activate Prior Knowledge

Use the charts to review the definitions of easy books, just-right books, and interesting books, and what your students have learned about choosing books.

Model the Lesson

Begin the lesson by handing out a book bag or book box to each student:

Readers, today is a very exciting day! You will be picking your own books to read for the week. I have special bags (boxes) with your names on them. Once you have selected your books, you get to keep them in your book bag.

Share your own book choices for the week:

Let me show you my book choices for the week: two easy books, two just-right books, and two interesting books. These two books are old favorites, and they are my easy books. I read them every year and never get tired of them. My just-right books are my two new teacher books. I am reading them to learn how to be a better reading teacher. Just like you, I sometimes get stuck on tricky words, but I am not worried about that because I know how to use fix-up strategies. My two interesting books are about dinosaurs. We are going to study them in science later, so I thought I better learn more about them, including why they became extinct.

Then inform students that you are so excited about your interesting books that you are going to read them first today.

Focus the Conversation

Ask partners to go knee-to-knee, eye-to-eye, and discuss whether they disagree with your decision to read the interesting books first. Introduce the concept of the weekly conversation skill focus:

When scholars disagree, they do it politely so they don't hurt feelings. If you name what you disagree with and tell why, the other person is usually more than willing to think about what you said. How you sound is important, too. If your tone is respectful, your partner will probably not be offended when you disagree.

This should make for a lively discussion. Students have heard many times that they should read their easy books first to build fluency, their just-right books next so they get better at reading, and their interesting books last. Listen to the conversations and encourage polite disagreements. Invite a few students to replay their conversations and show how they handled their disagreements.

Restate the Teaching Point

Review the reasons for reading books: to build fluency, to get better at reading, and to enjoy something they find interesting.

➤ Move to Independent Practice

Remind students that they get to select two books from each category and then check in with you when they have chosen their books. If necessary, review the order in which the books are read: easy, just-right, and interesting. Also, emphasize that they will be keeping these books in their book bags (or book boxes) and reading them for the entire week. Assure students that you will be available to assist them with book choice if they need any help. Distribute sticky notes so students can collect evidence of the fix-up strategies they have used to solve unfamiliar words in their just-right books.

INDEPENDENT READING PRACTICE

Students read books of their choice for 35–45 minutes using sticky notes as they read their just-right books. As you observe them, look for students to share this work later.

SHARE CIRCLE

Have students share their sticky-note evidence to demonstrate that they were able to solve tricky words using a fix-up strategy.

Lesson 22

Fix-Up Strategies

Teaching Point: Readers use fix-up strategies to predict and confirm tricky words.

Weekly Conversational Skill Focus: Disagreeing

Materials:
- Fix-Up Strategies chart
- display copy of continuous text
- sticky notes

Preparation:
- This lesson is a repeat of Lesson 17, Part 2, playing the How Many Ways of Knowing? game. Review the directions for the game on page 31.
- Cover five words in the text. Leave the initial sound, blend, or digraph uncovered.
- Allot approximately 35–45 minutes for students to read independently.

Building Independent Readers © 2012 by Linda Lee & Mary Haymond • Scholastic Teaching Resources

Activate Prior Knowledge

Review the list of reading strategies on the Fix-Up Strategies chart. Remind students how they can use the strategies to predict and confirm unknown words. Reread the last two strategies on the chart:

✮ Ask someone.

✮ Always ask: Does it make sense? Does it sound right? Does it look right?

Point out that students are still learning how to predict and confirm when they come to a tricky word in a book.

 Model the Lesson

Begin the How Many Ways of Knowing game. As you read the text, stop at each covered word and model how to use fix-up strategies to predict and confirm it. Write students' responses on a sticky note. Here's an example:

Teacher: *Watch and listen as I read. When I come to a tricky word, I will ask you to predict what the word could be and then confirm the prediction using fix-up strategies. I am stuck on this word. Abisai, what is your prediction?*

Abisai: *I predict that the word is* quickly.

Teacher: *Which fix-up strategy or strategies did you use?*

Abisai: *I reread and got my mouth ready, and that word came out.*

Teacher: *How can you confirm your prediction?*

Abisai: *I read the entire sentence. The word makes sense in the sentence. It looks and sounds right: "The young boy ran home as quickly as he could go."*

Uncover the word and match it to the one you wrote on the sticky note. Remember to record the fix-up strategies that students used in code, too. Continue the game until you reach the end of the book.

 Focus the Conversation

Invite partners to have a conversation by asking each other if there was anything in the lesson that they disagreed with or didn't understand. Listen to the partners' discussions to capture one that includes a disagreement or a discussion of something that needs to be clarified. Invite those students to replay their conversation for their peers. Clarify any misconceptions.

 Restate the Teaching Point

Tell students that playing the How Many Ways of Knowing game helps them use fix-up strategies to predict and confirm unfamiliar words.

 Move to Independent Practice

Distribute sticky notes and remind students to record evidence of the fix-up strategies they use when reading their just-right books. Tell them to be prepared to share their good work at share circle. Before sending students off to work independently, review the What's Helpful/What's Not Helpful chart with them.

INDEPENDENT READING PRACTICE

Students are now reading for approximately 35-45 minutes. Circulate around the room, conferring with readers about the fix-up strategies they are using. Note students who are displaying reading stamina and mention this at share circle.

SHARE CIRCLE

Invite students to share how they solved tricky words with fix-up strategies. Celebrate those who displayed reading stamina.

Lesson 23

Summary

Teaching Point: In a retell, readers tell the story and include important details. In a summary, readers tell the most important parts of the story.

Weekly Conversational Skill Focus: Disagreeing

Materials:
- Summary chart
- a display copy of *The Recess Queen* by Alexis O'Neill or the text that you used in Lesson 7
- What's Helpful/What's Not Helpful chart
- sticky notes

Preparation:
- Allot approximately 35–45 minutes for students to read independently.

 ## Activate Prior Knowledge

Read and review the elements of story grammar on the Summary chart.

 ## Model the Lesson

Introduce the focus of the lesson:

Today, I am going to teach you the difference between a retell and a summary. When readers retell a story, they provide every little detail they can remember in the right order. When readers summarize a story, they provide the most important parts. Summarizing text is what readers do most of the time.

Display the text. Retell the story. Then ask students to tell whether you gave a retelling or a summary. Give a summary of the story and repeat the process.

Building Independent Readers © 2012 by Linda Lee & Mary Haymond • Scholastic Teaching Resources

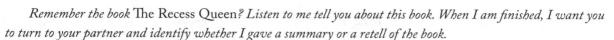

Remember the book The Recess Queen? *Listen to me tell you about this book. When I am finished, I want you to turn to your partner and identify whether I gave a summary or a retell of the book.*

Model a retell of the book and then model a summary.

 ## Focus the Conversation

Have students turn and talk to their partners about your modeling. Ask them to identify which was the retell and which was the summary and to discuss the reason for their decision.

 ## Restate the Teaching Point

Restate your teaching point for students:

When you summarize a text, you tell what is most important. Remember, this is what we did for our story-map mural of Owl Babies *and our story map of* The Little Red Hen. *When you give a retell, you include all the details in sequential order.*

 ## Move to Independent Practice

Tell students to be prepared to give an oral summary of one of their easy books or just-right books during share circle. Before students go off to read, ask them to think about the What's Helpful/What's Not Helpful chart and consider how they will apply those ideas to help create a positive work climate for themselves.

INDEPENDENT READING TIME

Now that students have their own book bags or book boxes and a way to hold their thinking with sticky notes, they can sustain approximately 35–45 minutes of independent reading. Therefore, they won't be doing any artistic responses for summary. The goal this week is for them to give an oral summary on an easy or just-right book.

SHARE CIRCLE

Introduce the activity Buzzing About Books:

From now on, I am going to give you a few minutes during share circle to talk about one of your books. We don't have enough time for everyone to share their good work during that time though, so we can also do an activity that gives everyone a chance to share. This activity is called "Buzzing About Books." At share circle, sit beside your partner. I will tell you that it is time for Buzzing About Books. You will have five minutes to talk together. I will always give you a focus for your discussion before you go off to read, just like I did today.

You must still be prepared to talk to the whole group when you come to share circle. Today, I asked you to be prepared to share a summary of one of your books. That's what I would like you to do right now. So, let's start Buzzing About Books. Turn to your partner and share!

Listen to the conversations and ask a few partners to share how Buzzing About Books went. Then ask one or two students to give an oral summary of one of their books.

Lesson 24

Summary

Teaching Point: A retell is something a teacher may ask readers to do at school. A summary is what readers do to help themselves understand and remember what they have read.

Weekly Conversational Skill Focus: Disagreeing

Materials
- Summary chart
- a display copy of *The Three Billy Goats Gruff* or the text you used in Lesson 5
- sticky notes
- What's Helpful/What's Not Helpful chart

Preparation:
- Allot 35–45 minutes for students to read independently.

 Activate Prior Knowledge

Review the difference between a summary and a retell. Expand on the differences between the two by discussing situations in which each one is appropriate:

Today, I am going to teach you when to give a retell and when to give a summary. It is important for you to know the difference between the two so you can be successful. Sometimes, to assess your reading, I give you a short book. While you read, I mark on a sheet of paper what you do when you come to a tricky word. This is one way of finding out how you use fix-up strategies. After you finish reading, I ask you to retell the story. I mark how many details you can tell me. These stories are short so it's simple to remember all the little details.

Summarizing text is what readers do most of the time. As you grow into reading chapter books, it will be important to carry the most important parts from one chapter to the next. It is also what readers do outside of school. When you want to tell a friend about a great book, you don't share all the details. You summarize the book by sharing the most important parts.

 Model the Lesson

Display the text. Remind students that you read it to them during the first week of school when they first learned about summarizing. Ask them to listen to you as you talk about the story. Begin by retelling the story. Then have partners turn and talk to discuss whether you gave them a retelling of the story or a summary. After the discussion, summarize the story for students. Again, have partners turn and talk to discuss whether you gave a retelling or a summary of the story.

Building Independent Readers © 2012 by Linda Lee & Mary Haymond • Scholastic Teaching Resources

Focus the Conversation

Ask pairs to discuss the difference between a retell and a summary. If they disagree, remind them to be polite and respectful and tell them to be sure to discuss how they can come to an agreement.

 ### Restate the Teaching Point

Reiterate the difference between retelling and summarizing and provide situations in which each would be appropriate.

 ### Move to Independent Practice

Tell students to be prepared to give an oral summary of one of their easy books or their just-right books during share circle. That's also what they'll be talking about with the partners during the Buzzing About Books period. Before sending students off to work independently, review the What's Helpful/ What's Not Helpful chart. Also, remind students to use sticky notes when they encounter an unfamiliar word in their reading.

INDEPENDENT READING PRACTICE

Students should be able to sustain their independent reading for 35–45 minutes. Again, they will need to be prepared to give an oral summary of an easy book or a just-right book in share circle.

SHARE CIRCLE

Review the procedure for the Buzzing About Books activity. Then have partners spend five minutes summarizing one of their books. Listen to the conversations and ask a few to share their summaries with the rest of the class.

Lesson 25

Summary

Teaching Point: Readers use a retell to tell a story in sequential order, including the details. Readers use a summary to tell the most important parts of a story.

Weekly Conversation Skill Focus: Disagreeing

Materials:
- Summary chart
- a display copy of a text that your students are familiar with, such as *The Ugly Duckling*

- sticky notes
- What's Helpful/What's Not Helpful chart

Preparation:
- Allot 35–45 minutes for students to read independently.

 ## Activate Prior Knowledge

Review the differences between a retell and a summary:

When someone retells a story, they provide every little detail they can remember in the right order. When someone summarizes a text, they share the most important parts.

 ## Model the Lesson

Note: This lesson is the same as Lesson 24, except that you use a different text. Display a copy of the text and ask students if they remember reading it. Have them listen as you talk about the story. Begin by retelling the story. Then have partners turn and talk to discuss whether you gave them a retelling of the story or a summary. After the discussion, summarize the story for students. Again, have partners turn and talk to discuss whether you gave a retelling or a summary of the story.

 ## Focus the Conversation

Ask pairs to discuss the difference between a retell and a summary. If they disagree, remind them to be sure to be respectful and to discuss how they can come to an agreement.

 ## Restate the Teaching Point

Reiterate the difference between retelling and summarizing and provide situations in which each would be appropriate.

 ## Move to Independent Practice

Tell students to be prepared to give an oral summary of one of their easy books or their just-right books during share circle. That's also what they'll be talking with the partners about during the Buzzing About Books period. Before sending students off to work independently, review the What's Helpful/ What's Not Helpful chart. Remind them to use their sticky notes when they encounter an unfamiliar word.

INDEPENDENT READING PRACTICE

Students should be able to sustain their independent reading for 35–45 minutes. Again, they will need to be prepared to give an oral summary on an easy book or a just-right book in share circle.

 Building Independent Readers © 2012 by Linda Lee & Mary Haymond • Scholastic Teaching Resources

SHARE CIRCLE

Review the procedure for the Buzzing About Books activity. Then have partners spend five minutes summarizing one of their books. Listen to the conversations and ask a few to share their summaries with the rest of the class.

Calendar for Lesson Plans
WEEK 6

LESSON 26

Book Choice: Find a just-right book to summarize

LESSON 27

Fix-Up Strategies: Monitor for meaning by predicting and confirming word choice.

LESSON 28

Summary: Reread a just-right book for a written summary

LESSON 29

Summary: Write a summary

LESSON 30

Summary: Share written summaries with a celebration

Lesson 26

Book Choice

Teaching Point: Readers read texts of different reading levels for a variety of purposes and in a variety of genres.

Weekly Conversation Skill Focus: Agreeing, adding on, asking questions, and disagreeing

Materials:
- Easy Books, Just-Right Books, and Interesting Books charts
- selection of books to model finding just-right books
- sticky notes

Preparation:
- Allot 45–50 minutes for students to read independently.

Overview: Preparation for Students' Written Summaries

Students will write a summary for a just-right book in Lesson 29 (Thursday). To ensure each child's success, Lessons 26–28 focus on the importance of being able to read and understand the just-right book before writing the summary. Again, it may sound unusual, but some students will attempt to write a summary for a story they haven't read, can't read, or don't understand. If they are reading chapter books, we recommend that one of their just-right book choices be limited to a short story this week. If your basal reading series has an anthology of short stories, allow students to choose one of them as a just-right text.

Some students will require extensive support to find narrative text that they can read and summarize in writing. Emergent readers may need to select books that have been read to them even though they are not quite able to read it independently. In our classrooms, we read books with repetition, rhyme, simple plots, few characters, and predictable structure during our daily read-aloud times. We have created a basket of books that we read and reread; they are available for emergent readers to select for a written summary. A list of some titles appears on page 36.

Activate Prior Knowledge

Read the Easy Books, Just-Right Books, and Interesting Books charts and review what students have learned about choosing books. Since students will choose their books for the week today, go over the criteria for selecting books for book bags or book boxes: two easy books, two just-right books, and one or two interesting books.

Model the Lesson

Explain that on Thursday, students will write a summary of one of their just-right books that they select today, so they should keep this in mind as they make their just-right book choices. Tell students that after hearing their oral summaries last week, you know they are ready to begin writing summaries.

Show students how you would select a just-right book to summarize in writing:

I have gathered some just-right books so I can find one I would like to write about. The first two are chapter books. It probably wouldn't be possible to finish a chapter book by Thursday, so I won't read either of these. The next two are nonfiction books. I could write information about the topic, but so far, we've only learned how to summarize stories, so nonfiction books won't work. This book might work. Let me sample a few pages and see if it is just right for me. If I can't read the words in the book, I won't understand what it is about. It would be impossible for me to write a summary.

Read aloud a few pages of the book and confirm that it is a good choice to summarize.

 # Focus the Conversation

Invite students to go knee-to-knee, eye-to-eye, and discuss why they should be thoughtful in choosing a just-right book to summarize. Listen to partners and try to capture a variety of conversations to serve as role models for all students. For example, try to find a partnership in which one partner added on to the comments made by the other, asked a question, or disagreed. As partners share their conversation with the rest of the class, name the conversational move they used.

 # Restate the Teaching Point

Share the following teaching point with students:

When you select your just-right books today, remember the importance of being able to read it because you are going to summarize it in writing.

 # Move to Independent Practice

Urge students to ask you if they need help in finding a just-right book to summarize. Also remind them to check in with you before they begin reading their book choices. Finally, explain that you will be looking for students who have reading stamina; they will get to select where they want to sit for independent reading practice tomorrow.

INDEPENDENT READING PRACTICE

Look over students' book selections and then send them to their table or desk to begin reading. Observe and record the names of a few who display reading stamina. Have students read independently for 45–50 minutes.

Building Independent Readers © 2012 by Linda Lee & Mary Haymond • Scholastic Teaching Resources

SHARE CIRCLE

Give students five minutes to buzz with their partner about the book they plan to summarize. Then compliment those who displayed reading stamina and explicitly identify the behaviors they exhibited. Ask those students to explain how they stayed focused:

These five students displayed amazing reading stamina. Here's what I saw them do: They stayed at their tables. They read their easy books first, their just-right books next, and their interesting books last. They focused on their reading and ignored distractions. Let's interview them to find out what made those behaviors possible!

Invite each student to talk about how he or she was able to exhibit reading stamina. Remind the class that these students get to choose where they want to sit tomorrow during independent reading practice.

Lesson 27

Fix-Up Strategies

Teaching Point: Readers use fix-up strategies and the How Many Ways of Knowing game to cross-check by predicting and confirming unfamiliar words.

Weekly Conversation Skill Focus: Agreeing, adding on, asking questions, and disagreeing

Materials:
- Fix-Up Strategies chart
- display copy of continuous text
- individual whiteboards for students to record their thinking
- sticky notes

Preparation:
- Cover three words in the text with sticky notes. Leave the first letter, blends, or digraphs uncovered so you can use "get your mouth ready" as a fix-up strategy.

 ## Activate Prior Knowledge

Review the list of reading strategies on the Fix-Up Strategies chart. Remind students how they can use the strategies to predict and confirm unfamiliar words. In preparation for playing the How Many Ways of Knowing game, reread the two strategies at the bottom of the chart:

✿ Ask someone.
✿ Always ask: Does it make sense? Does it sound right? Does it look right?

Model the Lesson

Explain how students will use individual whiteboards to play the game:

You all are getting so good at predicting and confirming tricky words. I thought I would give you all a chance to try this on a whiteboard. Here is how we will play the How Many Ways of Knowing game today. When we come to the covered word, write your prediction on the whiteboard. Use your best spelling so you will know what word you wrote. Then practice confirming the word with the other strategies. Let's see if everyone can confirm their prediction with four other strategies.

Read the book and stop at each covered word. Give students a few moments to write down their predictions and how they confirmed the predictions. Ask a few to share.

 ## Focus the Conversation

Invite pairs of students to have a conversation about whether using the whiteboards helped them focus on the lesson. Listen to partners to capture a conversation that includes a discussion of something that they disagreed on, agreed on, or questioned. Invite these pairs to replay their conversation for their peers and name the conversational moves they used.

 ## Restate the Teaching Point

Point out that playing this version of the How Many Ways of Knowing game challenges students to use more fix-up strategies to predict and confirm tricky words.

 ## Move to Independent Practice

Remind students to reread the just-right book they are going to write a summary for on Thursday. Let those who showed reading stamina in Lesson 26 choose where they want to read and work independently. Tell the rest of the class that you'll be observing them today to see who else is ready for this privilege tomorrow. Before students go to work, review the What's Helpful/What's Not Helpful chart.

INDEPENDENT READING PRACTICE

Circulate around the room, giving assistance to those who need help with the just-right book they are going to summarize. Also make note of students who are displaying reading stamina.

SHARE CIRCLE

Give pairs five minutes to orally summarize the just-book they will write about. Then celebrate students who showed reading stamina and ask them to share how they were able to keep their focus. Let them know that they will be able to choose where to work and read independently tomorrow.

Lesson 28

Summary

Teaching Point: Readers write a summary to improve their memory and their ability to recall important information as they read.

Weekly Conversation Skill Focus: Agreeing, adding on, asking questions, and disagreeing

Materials:
- chart paper, marker
- Summary chart
- text from Lesson 26
- Reading Comprehension Strategies Rubric: Summarizing Fiction (page 35)

Preparation:
- Create the Reading Comprehension Strategies Rubric: Summarizing Fiction.
- Allot 45–50 minutes for students to read independently.

 ## Activate Prior Knowledge

Use the Summary chart to review what students have learned about summary.

 ## Model the Lesson

Display the just-right book you selected in Lesson 26 to read and summarize in writing. Model writing a summary to show the most important parts of the story in sequence. After completing the summary, consult the rubric to assess your success. As you read aloud your summary, check off the criteria in Level 3 of the rubric.

 ## Focusing the Conversation

Ask partners to talk about how they will balance the task of reading their easy, just-right, and interesting books with thinking about writing their summaries tomorrow. As pairs turn and talk, listen to their conversations and choose a pair who effectively planned how to balance their independent reading practice:

I heard Morgan and John share that they will start by reading their easy books to warm up their brains. Then they will reread the just-right book they are going to summarize. Morgan said she was going to read it twice! Then she will read her other just-right book. If she has time, she will linger over her interesting texts. She isn't sure she will have time!

Restate the Teaching Point

Point out the elements of a good summary and how using the rubric can help them write a successful summary.

 Move to Independent Practice

Remind students to read or reread their just-right books today so they can create a written summary for it tomorrow. Tell the class that you will be looking for students with reading stamina; they will earn the privilege of deciding where to sit tomorrow after completing their written summaries.

INDEPENDENT READING PRACTICE

Students read independently for 45–50 minutes. Offer assistance as needed and watch for those who display reading stamina.

SHARE CIRCLE

Have students use the first five minutes of share circle as a Buzzing About Books period. Ask them to discuss whether they are ready to write a summary tomorrow and to explain their reasons. Share the names of those who displayed reading stamina.

Lesson 29

Summary

Teaching Point: Readers use a written summary to improve their memory and their ability to recall details as they read.

Weekly Conversation Skill Focus: Agreeing, adding on, asking questions, and disagreeing

Materials:
- Summary chart
- paper and pencils

 Activate Prior Knowledge

Use the Summary chart to review what students have learned about a summary:

Readers, today you get to prove that you can carry the important parts of a story in your head by writing a summary. It would be wise to reread the book you selected before you begin writing. It may take you the

entire independent reading time to read your book and complete your summary, but that's okay. This is a proud moment for you. Tomorrow, you will get to read your summary to your friends. This will be a celebration of all you've learned.

There is no teacher modeling in this lesson; responsibility is handed over to students.

 ## Focusing the Conversation

Ask partners to turn and talk about the important job they have to do today and what they are going to do first during independent reading practice. Listen to conversations and choose a pair to highlight:

I heard Allison and James share that they will start by rereading the book they selected to summarize. When they finish reading it, they will write the summary. If they get that done, they asked me if it would be okay to linger over their interesting texts. Of course, that would be a terrific idea! Writing a summary takes a great deal of effort, so cooling the brain down after all that work is fine.

 ## Restate the Teaching Point

Restate the important parts of a summary and the steps that students will need to take to write one: Reread their just-right book before summarizing and then write down the important points in it.

 ## Move to Independent Practice

Have students sit at their table or desk to write their summary. Those who earned the privilege of choosing where to sit yesterday can do so after completing their summary.

INDEPENDENT READING TIME

Students reread their book and write a summary. Circulate to provide assistance as needed. Watch for students displaying stamina!

SHARE CIRCLE

For today's Buzzing About Books activity, invite students to share how writing a summary helped them remember what they read. Don't have students share those summaries yet because not everyone may have finished writing. If some students finished in time to read their other books, celebrate those who displayed reading stamina and have them share what helped them focus. They get to choose where to sit tomorrow for independent reading practice!

Lesson 30

Summary

Teaching Point: Readers use a written summary to improve their ability to recall important details as they read.

Weekly Conversation Skill Focus: Agreeing, adding on, asking questions, and disagreeing

Materials:
- Summary chart
- Students' written summaries
- Reading Comprehension Strategies Rubric: Summarizing Fiction
- Speaking and Listening chart (see page 64)
- apple juice and cups or other celebratory treats

Preparation:
- Allot 20 minutes for students to read their summaries to each other.

 ## Activate Prior Knowledge

Use the Summary chart to review what students have learned about summarizing. Also celebrate their learning over the last six weeks.

Readers, today we are going to have a celebration! You have accomplished so much in the last six weeks. You have developed reading stamina, made wise book choices, and figured out tricky words. I can see that you are carrying important parts of a story in your head with your written summaries. I am so impressed! You have also learned how to have conversations about books.

 ## Focusing the Conversation

Display the Speaking and Listening chart so everyone can see it. Explain that pairs will read their summaries to each other and then discuss them. After that discussion, each partner will find someone else to read their summary to:

Now, readers, you are going to partner up and read your summaries to each other. You know that when you talk with someone, you look at the person who is talking and focus on what he or she is saying. When you finish, your partner will sign his or her name on the back of your summary. Then off you go to find a new partner to read your summary to.

Building Independent Readers © 2012 by Linda Lee & Mary Haymond • Scholastic Teaching Resources

Restate Your Teaching Point

Reiterate that a written summary improves readers' ability to recall details about what they have read. Students will also have focused conversations about their written summaries in which they may agree, add on, ask questions, and/or disagree appropriately in response.

 Move to Independent Practice

This reading and discussing activity will last for about 20 minutes. After students do this, allow them to cozy up to their books and read for the duration of the time. Allot 45-50 minutes for students to read independently.

INDEPENDENT READING PRACTICE

Today's event should relate an important message to the students. You think it is a very big deal that they have learned so much and are now able to read independently for such a long time. This will set the stage for successful independent reading for the rest of the year.

Collect the written summaries and use the rubric to evaluate students' learning—and your own teaching!

SHARE CIRCLE

When students gather on the carpet for share circle, toast their success with cups of apple juice or another treat. Then ask partners to turn and talk about how they have grown as readers. Single out conversations to share with the rest of the class:

I heard Connor and Chenoa talk about how they spend most of their time reading their just-right books. Chenoa said it was fun for her because she liked figuring out tricky words with her fix-up strategies. Connor noticed he sounded more like a storyteller because he never forgot to practice his easy books first. Clayton, Maria, Maud, and Eva talked about how they loved to sit in the rocking chairs and read.

● ● ●

You and your students have worked hard to create an effective learning environment and employ the strategies and skills necessary for a successful independent reading program. The pacing of your lessons may differ from the one presented here, but your results should be the same. Now your energies can be focused on instruction rather than on managing student behavior during independent reading time. Your students are taking responsibility for their learning and happily engaging with reading for long periods of time. You are giving them a gift that will last a lifetime!

References

Professional

Allington, R. (2006). *What really matters for struggling readers: Designing research-based programs* (2nd ed.). Boston: Pearson/Allyn & Bacon.

Allington, R. (2002). What I've learned about effective reading instruction from a decade of studying exemplary elementary classroom teachers. *Phi Delta Kappan*, 83(10), 740–747.

Angelillo, J. (2003). *Writing about reading: From book talk to literary essays, grades 3–8*. Portsmouth, NH: Heinemann.

Armbruster, B., Anderson, T., & Ostertag, J. (1987). Does text structure/summarization instruction facilitate learning from expository text? *Reading Research Quarterly, 22*, 331–346.

Baumann, J. F., & Bergeron, B. (1993). Story-map instruction using children's literature: Effects on first graders' comprehension of central narrative elements. *Journal of Reading Behavior, 25*, 407–437.

Cole, A. D. (2003). *Knee to knee, eye to eye: Circling in on comprehension.* Portsmouth, NH: Heinemann

Collins, K. (2004). *Growing readers: Units of study in the primary classroom.* Portland, ME: Stenhouse

Davis, Z. T. (1994). Effects of prereading story mapping on elementary readers' comprehension. *Journal of Educational Research, 87*(6), 353–360.

Fielding, L., & Pearson, D. P. (1994). Reading comprehension: What works. *Educational Leadership, 62–68.*

Guthrie, J. T., Schafer, W. D., Wang, Y. Y., & Afflerbach, P. (1995). Relationships of instruction of reading: An exploration of social, cognitive, and instructional connections. *Reading Research Quarterly, 30*, 8–25.

Harvey, S., & Goudvis, A. (2007). *Strategies that work: Teaching comprehension for understanding and engagement* (2nd ed.). Portland, ME: Stenhouse.

Harvey, S., & Goudvis, A. (2009). *The primary comprehension toolkit: Language and lessons for active literacy.* Portsmouth, NH: Heinemann.

Keene, E., & Zimmerman, S. (2007). *Mosaic of thought: The power of comprehension strategy instruction* (2nd ed.). Portsmouth, NH: Heinemann.

Keene, E. O. (2008). *To understand: New horizons in reading comprehension.* Portsmouth, NH: Heinemann.

McGregor, T. (2009). *Comprehension connections: Bridges to strategic reading.* Portsmouth, NH: Heinemann.

Nichols, M. (2006). *Comprehension through conversation: The power of purposeful talk in the reading workshop.* Portsmouth, NH: Heinemann.

Paris, S., Wasik, B. A., & Turner, J. C. (1991). The development of strategic readers. In R. Barr, M. L. Kamil, P. B. Mosenthal, & P. D. Pearson (Eds.), *Handbook of reading research: Vol. 2.* 609–640. New York: Routledge.

Pearson, P. D., & Gallagher, M. C. (1983). The instruction of reading comprehension. *Contemporary Educational Psychology, 8*, 317–344.

Schunk, D.H., & Zimmerman, B.J. (1996). Developing self-efficacious readers and writers: The role of social and self-regulatory processes. In J. Guthrie & A. Wigfield (Eds.), *Reading engagement: Motivating readers through integrated instruction* (pp. 14–29). Newark, DE: International Reading Association.

Szymusiak, K., Sibberson, F., & Koch, L. (2008). *Beyond leveled books: Supporting early and transitional readers in grades K–5* (2nd ed.). Portland, ME: Stenhouse.

Children's Literature

Bloom, Becky. (1999). *Wolf!* New York: Orchard.

Crews, Donald. (1996). *Shortcut*. New York: Greenwillow.

Frazee, Marla. (2006). *Walk on! A guide for babies of all ages*. Orlando: Harcourt.

Galdone, Paul. (2001). *The Three Billy Goats Gruff*. New York: Clarion.

Jordan, Deloris, & Jordan, Roslyn M. (2000). *Salt in his shoes: Michael Jordan in pursuit of a dream*. New York: Simon & Schuster.

Krull, Kathleen. (1996). *Wilma unlimited: How Wilma Rudolph became the world's fastest woman*. San Diego: Harcourt Brace.

Martin, Jr., Bill, & John Archambault, (1989). *Chicka chicka boom boom*. New York: Simon & Schuster.

McQueen, Lucinda. (1985). *The little red hen*. New York: Scholastic.

O'Neill, Alexis. (2002). *The recess queen*. New York: Scholastic.

Pilkey, Dav. (1996). *Dragon Tales*. New York: Scholastic.

Shannon, David. (1998). *No, David!* New York: Blue Sky.

Steig, William. (1986). *Brave Irene*. New York: Farrar, Straus, Giroux.

Waddell, Martin. (1992). *Owl babies*. Cambridge, MA: Candlewick.

Willems, Mo. (2007). *There is a bird on your head!* New York: Hyperion.

Winter, Jeanette. (2005). *The librarian of Basra: A true story from Iraq*. Orlando: Harcourt.

Winter, Jeanette. (2008). *Wangari's trees of peace: A true story from Africa*. Orlando: Harcourt.

Professional Resources

Allen, P. (2009). *Conferring: The keystone of a readers' workshop*. Portland ME: Stenhouse.

Allington, R., & Johnston, P. (2002) *Reading to learn: Lessons from exemplary fourth-grade classrooms*. New York: Guilford.

Calkins, L. (2001). *The art of teaching reading*. New York: Longman.

Cambourne, B. (1988). *The whole story: Natural learning and the acquisition of literacy in the classroom*. New York: Scholastic.

Duffy, G. G. (2003). *Explaining reading: A resource for teaching concepts, skills, and strategies*. New York: Guilford.

Guthrie, J., Schafer, W., & Huang, C. (2001). Benefits of opportunity to read and balanced instruction on the NAEP. *Journal of Educational Research, 96*, 145–162.

Krashen, S. (2001). More smoke and mirrors: A critique of the National Reading Panel report on fluency. *Phi Delta Kappan, 83*(2)119–123.

Miller, D. (2002). *Reading with meaning: Teaching comprehension in the primary grades*. Portland, ME: Stenhouse.

Miller, D. (2008). *Teaching with intention: Defining beliefs, aligning practice, taking action, K–5*. Portland, ME: Stenhouse.

Mooney, M. E. (1988). *Developing life-long readers*. Wellington, New Zealand: Ministry of Education.

Mooney, M. E. (1990). *Reading to, with, and by children*. Katonah, NY: Richard C. Owen Publishers.

Peterson, R. (1992). *Life in a crowded place: Making a learning community*. Portsmouth, NH: Heinemann.

Power, B. M., & Hubbard, R. (Eds.). (1991). *The Heinemann reader: Literacy in process*. Portsmouth, NH: Heinemann.

Pressley, M., & Wharton-McDonald, R. (1997). Skilled comprehension and its development through instruction. *School Psychology Review, 26*, 448–466.

Routman, R. (2003). *Reading essentials: The specifics you need to teach reading well*. Portsmouth, NH: Heinemann.

Stanovich, K.E. (2002). *Progress in understanding reading: Scientific foundations and new frontiers*. New York: Guilford.

Taberski, S. (2000). *On solid ground: Strategies for teaching reading, K–3*. Portsmouth, NH: Heinemann.

Wang, J. H., & Guthrie, J. T. (2004). Modeling the effects of intrinsic motivation, extrinsic motivation, amount of reading, and past reading achievement on text comprehension between U.S. and Chinese students. *Reading Research Quarterly, 39*(2), 162–186.

Appendix

Just-Right Books for First Grade

Look What I Can Do by Jose Aruego
A Dark, Dark Tale by Ruth Brown
I Like Books by Anthony Browne
Dear Zoo by Rod Campbell
Biscuit series by Alyssa Capucilli
Do You Want to Be My Friend? by Eric Carle
Have You Seen My Cat? by Eric Carle
Go Dog, Go! by P. D. Eastman
The Chick and the Duckling by Mirra Ginsburg
Where's Spot? by Eric Hill
Look! Look! Look! By Tana Hoban
Changes, Changes by Pat Hutchins
Rosie's Walk by Pat Hutchins
Brown Bear, Brown Bear, What Do You See?
    by Bill Martin, Jr.
Chicka Chicka Boom Boom by Bill Martin, Jr.
Just Like Me by Barbara Neasi
Mary Wore Her Red Dress by Merle Peek
Goodnight Gorilla by Peggy Rathmann
No! David series by David Shannon
Have You Seen the Crocodile? by Colin West
Cat on the Mat by Brian Wildsmith
Elephant and Piggie series by Mo Willems
I Went Walking by Sue Williams
Mama by Jeanette Winter
Dig, Dig by Leslie Wood

Just-Right Books for Second Grade

Young Cam Jansen series by David A. Adler
Fly Guy series by Tedd Arnold
Are You My Mother? by P. D. Eastman
Hattie and the Fox by Mem Fox
Ready Freddy series by Abby Klein
Frog and Toad series by Arnold Lobel
Mouse Soup by Arnold Lobel
Put Me in the Zoo by Robert Lopshire
Fox series by James Edward Marshall
Just Me and My Puppy by Mercer May
There's a Nightmare in My Closet by Mercer Mayer
Little Bear series by Else Holmelund Minarik
Magic Tree House series by Mary Pope Osborne

Dragon's Fat Cat series by Dav Pilkey
Ricky Ricotta series by Dav Pilkey
Henry and Mudge series by Cynthia Rylant
Mr. Putter and Tabby series by Cynthia Rylant
Poppleton series by Cynthia Rylant
Hop on Pop by Dr. Seuss
Nate the Great series by Marjorie Weinman Sharmat
The Bailey School Kids (Jr. Chapter Books series)
    by Marcia Thorton and Debbie Dadey
Elephant and Piggie series by Mo Willems
Pigeon series by Mo Willems
The Napping House by Audrey Wood
The Teeny Tiny Woman by Harriet Ziefert

Just-Right Trade Books for Third Grade

Cam Jansen series by David A. Adler
Roscoe Riley series by Katherine Applegate
Mr. and Mrs. Green series by Keith Baker
Ivy and Bean series by Annie Barrows and Sophie Blackall
Flat Stanley series by Jeff Brown
Bad Kid series by Nick Bruel
Stories Julian Tells series by Ann Cameron
Amber Brown series by Paula Danziger
Pee Wee Scout series by Judy Denton
Jackson Friends series by Michelle Edwards
Polk Street series by Patricia Reilly Giff
A to Z Mysteries series by Ron Roy and John Steven Gurney
Max Malone series by Charlotte Herman and Cat Bowman Smith
Pinky and Rex series by James Howe
Horrible Harry series by Suzy Kline
Meg MacKintosh series by Lucinda Landon
Fables by Arnold Lobel
Stink series by Megan McDonald and Peter H. Reynolds
Junie B. Jones series by Barbara Park
Clementine series by Sara Pennypacker
The Littles series by John Peterson
Marvin Redpost series by Louis Sachar
Bailey School Kids series by Marcia Thorton Jones and
    Debbie Dadey
Geronimo Stilton series
Ranger Rick magazine

A range of nonfiction leveled books from publishers, such as Scholastic, Rigby, Newbridge, National Geographic, are available for just-right book choices.

Building Independent Readers © 2012 by Linda Lee & Mary Haymond • Scholastic Teaching Resources